TWO FOR THE ROAD

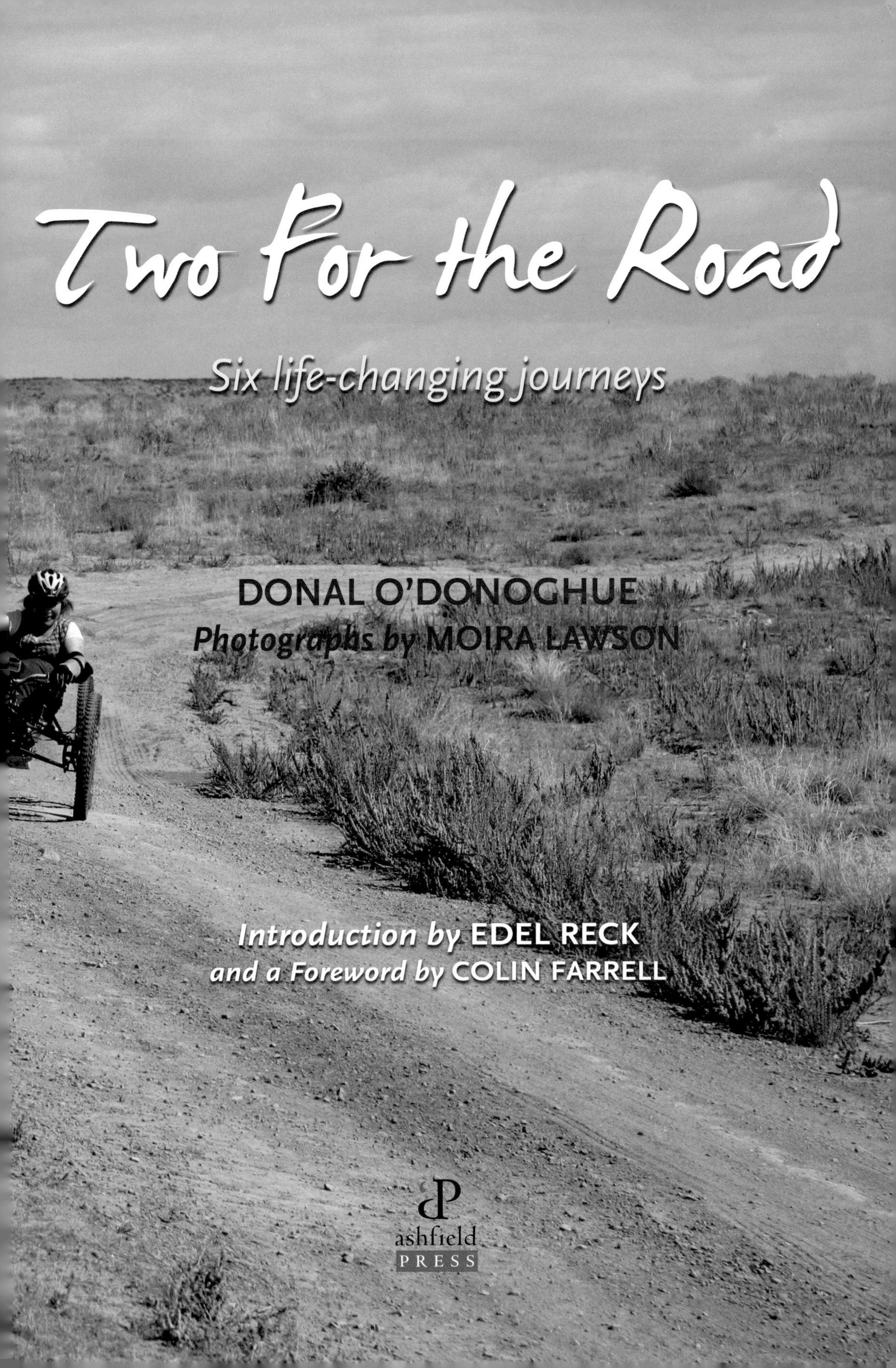

Two For the Road

Six life-changing journeys

DONAL O'DONOGHUE

Photographs by MOIRA LAWSON

Introduction by EDEL RECK
and a Foreword by COLIN FARRELL

ashfield
PRESS

Published in 2011 by

ASHFIELD PRESS • DUBLIN • IRELAND

© Donal O'Donoghue 2011
© Photographs – Moira Lawson
(except Chapter One – from collection of Edel Reck)

ISBN: 978-1-901658-83-5

This book is designed and typeset by SUSAN WAINE
in 11.5 on 14 point Scala
Printed in Ireland

Contents

Foreword

I HAVE NEVER MET EDEL RECK. I have never heard her voice. And yet, I feel honoured to know her. My knowledge of Edel, and her tireless work on behalf of herself and others, comes by way of an e-mail friendship we struck up in the last year or so.

When she first told me about the concept for *Two For the Road* I was blown away. It was clear that Edel had touched on a real and tangible structure by which to set forth, in the most entertaining and wide-reaching way her belief that disability is not the end of the road. In fact, Edel's disability has inspired her to look at the world and her place in it and make her mark. It has inspired her, led by her strength of spirit, to pave that road boldly and brilliantly.

I can't imagine what it has been like for Edel to live her life with spina bifida. I say that with compassion not pity. I imagine there have been times of great hardship, both physical and emotional. I have a feeling that bias has been faced. Knowing Edel through her words and deeds, I also have a feeling that bias does not last long in her company. I really have no idea of how it is for any man or woman to live the lives they live, but sometimes, just sometimes, I – and I think we, as a people – get inspiration from what we see in each other.

I become inspired when I think of Edel Reck and the monumental task that she has moulded into her life's purpose. This television series and book being two of those chapters.

By sharing with us the many daring duos on *Two For the Road,* and by taking us through her experience in this accompanying book, she is not letting us in on what it means to be disabled, but what it means to be alive. She is showing us, sharing with us, that many times in life we are confined only by the mind, even if our bodies seem to be screaming 'No' the loudest.

It's 6:22am and the sun is rising over a sleepy Toronto City. I have just looked at Edel Recks facebook account. Her profile has her favourite athletes listed, Eamonn Coghlan, Ken Doherty, Sonia O'Sullivan. Her favorite books are human interest. Her favorite television shows are documentaries and travel. Most tellingly of all are her interests and activities. They are listed as canoeing, alpine skiing, travelling, cooking, snooker and athletics!!

Oh, that I were that active. This is not the profile of a person who lives within set limits.

I hope people find their way to this book. I hope the television show brings them here. I hope Edel keeps advocating. I hope she keeps climbing mountains and screaming from them. Her voice is persistent and wise and it is a voice for change. Essential, life-affirming change.

This is a book about Edel and others lives.
This is a book about ability.

TORONTO 2011

Colin Farrell

Introduction

STEVIE WONDER once said that 'You can't base your life on other people's expectations'. That just about sums up my philosophy. I believe that people are only limited by their own imagination, that life really is a blank canvas on which dreams can be fulfilled in living, vibrant colour through application, determination and, most importantly, self belief.

From the seed of a single idea – pairing a person who has a disability with a celebrity companion for a trailblazing journey of discovery – *Two For the Road* grew into a wonderful adventure that did indeed surpass people's expectations. Turning the dream into reality was a challenge, but as those close to me will tell you, I do relish a challenge! The result has been worth all the effort and all the little anxieties that such an undertaking inevitably brings. To paraphrase Henry Ford, the setbacks we endure help us in our marching onward.

I hope that *Two For the Road* will in some small way help to break down the barriers created by attitudes towards people with a disability. People often describe me as being confined to a wheelchair and I don't really see it that way. With my wheelchair I have freedom and feel liberated; without it I'm confined. I have always believed that it's far better to be outdoors trying new things, than sitting at home wondering what I'm missing out on. I embrace the outdoor life and all it has to offer. It makes me feel alive and free. The earth's rich landscapes, from mountains and forests to rivers and oceans, are for everyone to experience and enjoy and I have always been a strong advocate for inclusion. Those of us who have a disability can do and want to do most things just like anyone else, but sometimes we just do them in a different way. And yes, there IS a way. I hope that this book and accompanying television series, not only communicate that message, but also inspire others to follow their dreams, whatever obstacle is in their path.

Two For the Road could not have succeeded without the help and support of a great many people. The first person is Steve Carson, Director of Programmes – RTÉ Television. Once I had his backing I spoke with independent production company, Yellow Asylum Films, whose directors Martin Mahon and Alan Gilsenan had many meetings with Commissioning Editors in RTÉ in an attempt to bring my vision onto the small screen. I thank them both for their support, commitment and professionalism and the entire crew including Moira Lawson, Kieran Horgan, Richard Kendrick, Oliver Fallen as well as those behind the scenes who helped create a bit of magic. Without them this would not have happened. I would also like to acknowledge the support of Mick McCarthy, Former Head of Features RTÉ TV; Heather Parsons, Former Editor, *RTÉ Guide*; Susan Waine and John Davey at Publishers, Ashfield Press. Donal O'Donoghue, Features Editor of the *RTÉ Guide* and author of this book, has been a true friend over the years and accompanied me on many of my adventures. I thank him for his backing, his company and his patience. Thanks must also go to Colin Farrell who has been fulsome in his support of the project. Hollywood stars are forever in demand and I am indebted to Colin for devoting his valuable time to the venture. A word of thanks too for Jim Hayes, Deputy Group Editor at *People Newspapers* in Wexford, for his enthusiastic support and help in creating awareness through the newspaper group. Finally, I would like to pay tribute to my friends and family – dad John, mam Eileen, brother Des, his late wife Karen and their three children Cliona, Cian and Caitlin.

Edel Reck
June, 2011

CHAPTER ONE

Climb Every Mountain (and then ski down it)

SOMEWHAT APPROPRIATELY it all started at a place called Loon Mountain. The small New Hampshire town, two hours drive north of Boston, is home to a ski resort in the winter months, one of many on the north eastern seaboard of the USA. What makes Loon Mountain special is that it also caters for skiers with physical/sensory disabilities. Skiers of all ages and abilities visit here, from those born with a disability to war veterans injured in conflicts in Iraq, Afghanistan and elsewhere. Some are absolute beginners, others can turn on a dime, but they all share the same passion for adventure and living life to the absolute max.

One day in February 2002, a motley crew assembled at the foot of Loon Mountain, named not because the local village has an above average quota of idiots but for the local bird with the distinctive plaintive cry. At the head of the small party was Edel Reck, a Wexford woman, who had been born with spina bifida and was a wheelchair-user since her early teens. With her was fellow county person, Shane McDonagh, who was also born with spina bifida, and me: the journalist. Through the previous week Reck, by then a reasonably competent skier, was introducing her colleague to the thrill of skiing the white hills of New Hampshire. Tentative, nervous beginnings had given way to fun and some skill. Now it was the turn of the journalist to try adaptive skiing.

Having only recently mastered the more orthodox art of downhill skiing or even standing upright on skis, this was a new departure. So it was with justifiable anxiety that the instructor eyed up the hack as Edel Reck cajoled him into something that looked like a sleeping bag on skis. The conversation went something like this.

You've got to try it!
Why?
Because I want to see how you cope.
Why?
Because it could be fun.
Why?
Go on, just do it for God's sake.
Er, why?

Of course the journalist lost. Or won. Depending on your perspective. And so ended up shoehorning himself into that sleeping bag with skis underneath before being handed a pair of paddles(outriggers) to steer. Left paddle, left turn. Right paddle, right turn. No paddle, fall over! The best that can be said about those initial moments is that being close to the ground you don't have far to fall. Even so it was decided, in the interests of safety (not only the journalist's but all other skiers) that this maiden (and final) voyage as an adaptive skiier be conducted on the nursery slopes. It was terrifying and exhilarating and utterly confusing all at the same time. The journalist managed the almost impossible of falling over ten times in less that twenty metres before coming to a shuddering halt (most of the shuddering was fear induced as the incline barely allowed the speed to go above 3 mph) at the bottom of the run.

As I struggled out of the contraption, I noticed that Edel Reck had a curious glint in her eye. What I didn't know then was that yet another ambitious notion was germinating in that hyperactive mind. A few weeks later, back in Ireland and far away from skis and snow, Reck phoned with a suggestion. What about a book chronicling a series of adventures in which a physically disabled person and an able-bodied person embarked on an adventure together. That intriguing premise was tossed into the air and juggled through a number of combinations. What fell to earth was this. The two adventurers would have to get from A to B but the catch was that the able-bodied person would have to use the same specialised adaptive equipment, or be physically restricted in some way, to mimic the conditions and situation of their travelling companion.

It was a novel idea that promised an adventure for the heart but also for the mind as both people would, in the course of their physical endeavours, be seeing the world anew – in essence through each others eyes. It would be a travel book with quite a few differences. That was the theory. Along the way the ambitions expanded to the notion of making it into a TV series. Reck was, as she always was, confident of achieving the goal. It was to prove one of her toughest challenges

Some nine years – and many rejections – later that idea is a book based on the TV series, *Two For the Road*. The series was made by Yellow Asylum Films for RTÉ and the Broadcasting Authority of Ireland, with Alan Gilsenan directing and Martin Mahon producing. The six part series features a number of people who have endured their own epic journeys through life and against many odds, from the actor David Proud (*Desperados, EastEnders*), who was born with spina bifida to the former Irish Minister, Seán Connick, the first wheelchair user in Dáil Éireann. Sharing the adventures and challenges are familiar faces such as the accordion player Sharon Shannon, comedienne Maeve Higgins and the former snooker world champion, Ken Doherty. And of course the series also includes the person it all began with, Edel Reck.

By any yardstick, Edel is an impressive person. She is also very persuasive, very stubborn and very determined. For a long time she has nursed a dream. A number of dreams in fact. Such tenacity comes from a life lived through adversity where nothing comes easy. "I always believed that there is no such thing as the impossible," she says. "Although I was born with spina bifida, and have been a wheelchair-user since my teens, I have been lucky enough to do things that many able-

bodied people can only dream of. I have trekked to the top of Machu Picchu, I have skied the Rockies, I have gone horse riding in the Mojave Desert and I have sailed the Mediterranean in a tall ship."

I first met Edel Reck at Dublin airport in February 1997. On that morning the departures area was the usual carousel of chaos with hordes of holidaymakers hauling baggage and expectations towards check-in desks. In the middle of the melee, located near the line for the flights to the Canary Islands, was a group from Spina Bifida and Hydrocephalus Association, Ireland. The ambulant participants and wheelchair users, along with their friends, looked like an oasis of calm. I was there as a journalist to report on a TV documentary that was being made to chronicle this week-long trip. Our ultimate destination was Las Palmas in Gran Canaria where the tall ship, the *STS Lord Nelson*, was moored.

The *Lord Nelson* is an unique ship. Built under the auspices of the Jubilee Sailing Trust charity, it was purpose designed to enable people of all physical and sensory abilites to take an active role in sailing the ship (the *Lord Nelson* and its sister ship, *Tenacious*, are the only two Class A tall ships in the world thus built). After a shaky construction history, it embarked on its maiden voyage in October 1986. Since then the *Lord Nelson* and *Tenacious* have carried more than 34,000 people. Apart from its core permanent crew of professional seafarers, the so-called 'voyage crew' can be up to forty in number. On board also are a number of volunteers who do some of the heavy lifting and in turn are fed and watered and get to experience an extraordinary adventure.

I signed up for the 1997 trip because (a) it was free (b) it was The Canaries and (c) the boat had a bar. But there are no cheap rides on the *Lord Nelson*. Or as the official brochure prefers to put it, there are 'no passengers'. The moment you walk up the gangway you are handed a life-jacket and assigned to a watch. For the following week you are likely to work harder than you have done in a long time – from cleaning the heads (toilets) to preparing dinner, from 'flaking out' the anchor chain to raising the sail. You are also very likely to love every minute of it. But all that was on the distant horizon that hectic morning in Dublin airport. Right then most people were probably anticipating nothing more (or less) than a sun holiday on a boat (with a bar).

Except for one person. Somewhere in the midst of that huddle of Gran Canaria-bound landlubbers was Edel Reck. As the National Youth Officer with Spina Bifida & Hydrocephalus Ireland, the *Lord Nelson* trip was her baby and she didn't want it thrown out with the bath water. For many months she had initiated, organised and overseen the expedition and was also the PR guru, drumming up media support for a TV documentary, eventually to be titled *Against The Wind*, that would be shot during the week-long voyage.

Although she had masterminded one earlier voyage in December

– and that by all accounts was a storming success – Reck was not counting her chickens. Certainly that morning in the airport she was troubled by a spaghetti junction of unanswered questions. What if it was a plan too far? Would the other travellers, both disabled and able-bodied, enjoy the week as much as she knew that she would? Would the TV documentary ever get to see the light of a TV schedule?

By that time Reck was already a seasoned traveller, having criss-crossed the globe in pursuit of her other main hobby: athletics, attending Olympic Games and World Championship meetings as well as the occasional snooker tournament. But with the *Lord Nelson* she was venturing into uncharted waters. She needn't have worried. One week later the group were back in Dublin airport – waving goodbye with high fives and carrying with them memories of an unforgettable week on the high seas. There was an especially broad grin on Edel Reck's face. The trip proved the truth in her long-held philosophy: 'Confinement is only in one's mind' .

Edel Reck was born in Wexford General Hospital on February 19, 1968 with spina bifida (an incomplete development of the spinal cord). From the very beginning the odds were stacked against her. "The day after I was born I was transferred to The Richmond Hospital in Dublin for surgery on my back. As my mam had a Caesarean section, she never saw me immediately after the birth.

The following morning she saw a little child being lifted into the ambulance to be taken away not realising that it was me. She had never seen or held me at that point. In fact, I was in the Rich-mond for nearly three weeks during which time my mother never saw me. During those weeks my dad used to travel up to Dublin on the train to visit me."

Edel's parents are Eileen and John and she has one other sibling, a brother Des, three years older than her. She grew up just outside the town in a bungalow on New Line Road, where she lived until she was sixteen. Across the road was a large housing estate and many of her early friends, including her best buddy, Suzanne, lived there. Even then Edel didn't see herself as being any different from any other kid. "Absolutely not. My father built me a doll's house in which we would all congregate and play. I didn't feel any different at that time. I was treated just like any other child."

But her life was different and the first few years were pockmarked by a litany of hospital visits. "There were a number of surgeries to straighten my legs and lengthen them. My left leg is still four inches shorter than my right leg." There were also accidents (leg breaks, ankle breaks) and lonesome times spent far away from home. "My first ever memory was when I was about three years of age. I was in the Central Remedial Clinic in Clontarf. I remember my parents coming to see me and then later, when they would be trying to sneak away, I would scream the place down. My mother and my father would also be in tears as it was breaking their heart too."

She learnt to walk using crutches and callipers. It was trial and sometimes error. One time she tumbled down steps and damaged her baby teeth. "My legs were always dead weight but my arms were very strong and I was able to pull myself along, dragging my legs." Soon she was pretty nifty on her sticks and from the age of six would make the twenty minute trip to the local national school, Kennedy Park, accompanied by her mother. "It was all uphill in the morning and in the afternoon I would hop home through the fields. When I was about seven or eight I got a tricycle and so I would pedal to school with my mam."

Her father would take her

everywhere ("I was like his shadow") while her mother fussed over her, making sure that everything for her daughter was as good as it could be. "My mother was very protective of me and like many mothers and daughters we would argue a lot but that has made me the person I am today. I was always determined to do even the simple things like dressing myself or combing my hair. And if I didn't know how to do something or found it difficult, I wanted to learn how to do it and find a way. The thing is that the more people try to hold me back, the more I want to show that I can do different things to prove myself. It's very difficult living in a society where people constantly doubt your ability to do things.

In between the early hospital visits were the 'pilgrimages' to Lourdes, the Marian Shrine in the South West of France. Edel doesn't remember the first time but reckons she was barely two years old when her mother took her to the shrine. "On my third visit to Lourdes I fell and broke my ankle. My brother said afterwards that I went for a cure and came back worse." Not being especially religious, she didn't attach any significance to the visits. "I certainly wasn't praying even though I would be brought down to the grotto for the rosary. I went to Lourdes one more time with my mother.

All I remember of that time was not wanting to be there. The thing is that I was happy as I was. In my own head I wasn't any different from anyone else."

For Edel Reck there was always that need to prove herself: an insistent voice inside her head, railing against those who would, out of misguided empathy or otherwise, try to fence in her ambitions. "People would sometimes put you down, dismiss you and your dreams. But once people start being negative I just leave. Negativity brings you down.

She remembers details from the early days, vignettes to colour in how she grew in confidence and determination. Like the time she was wheeling on the street, drinking a coke, when an elderly woman dropped some change into the can in her hand. But slowly and surely she was gaining her independence. "There is one Saturday afternoon, when I was about fourteen, that I remember very clearly. On that afternoon my mam was doing her usual grocery shopping and my dad said, 'why don't we leave her off on her own?' It was the first time I was ever in the town by myself. From then on they would leave me go and do my own thing for a few hours every Saturday. That first time taught me that it was OK to ask for help because everyone needs help sometimes. I would ask someone for help to get into a shop rather than stay outside looking in. That also enabled me to learn the knack of getting up and down steps myself."

But it was her parents who made the move that was to shape her future. Quiet and unassuming in some ways, they were determined from the outset that their daughter would not be sent to a specialised school. At the relatively mature age of six, the delay due to those extended sojourns in hospital, Edel packed her school bag for the first time. "My parents had a battle trying to enroll me in Kennedy Park National school as the educational authorities wanted to wait until the new school was completed. But my parents were anxious that I start straight away as I was six years old and had missed enough already through illness."

So start she did and a few years later walked into the brand new national school under Principal, Sr Patricia. "Donal Thompson appointed a short time later was very inclusive. He treated me just like any other student which is how it should be. I didn't want to be treated any differently from anyone else. Being educated through the mainstream education system was crucial for me."

In her early teens she got a wheelchair. "As my bones started to become heavier it was more difficult to carry myself around on the crutches. The chair gave me greater mobility and thus more independence. I could also wear what I want as I wasn't restricted to wearing certain types of clothes or trying to hide callipers. But the biggest thing was that now I was able to keep up with everybody else. They didn't have to wait around for me any longer."

Even so, things were changing. Now she was in Secondary school friends from the early days began to drift away. Little gangs and cliques were formed and increasingly she was relegated to the fringes. "The other children weren't nasty but I did feel left out. At

break and lunch times for example they would all be in the yard, hanging out together and talking, and I would be sitting by myself. I used to get upset at times but I didn't let anybody see that. I'd just get on with it. But I would have been lonely at times feeling excluded. I don't know whether it was because I was slowing people down or what. But I have moved on and so have they."

So she joined the school's athletic club and signed up in the local choir. Sport was a natural outlet as it has always been big in the Reck home. Her mother was addicted to darts and snooker on the TV, her father was a GAA man and Edel was glued to the track and field events, especially athletics. "My first big memory of athletics was watching Eamonn Coghlan winning gold in the World Championships in Helsinki in 1983."

At the age of 15 she joined the local athletics club. My sports were the javelin, discus, shot putt and the 100 metres. I loved the javelin. It was the event I put the most effort into and it was also my best event. I started competing with the Irish Wheelchair Association Sport (IWA Sport). The Spina Bifida Association started getting involved with the Sports Club of the Irish Wheelchair Associaton."

Her first competition was in Clontarf at the Headquarters of the Irish Wheelchair Association. "I was a dead loss but I enjoyed it all the same and wanted to improve. My father would train with me in the evenings. The routine was that I would throw things – shot putt, javelin, discus – and he would measure the distance and of course fetch." When the Wexford Wheelchair Sports Club was established Reck trained there and began to build a new network of friends and compete in more competitions. "The games were important for me as I could compete but it was also a social outlet. I met Colette O'Reilly, an athlete who went onto greater things, at that time."

Edel Reck was 19 when she left school, having repeated 2nd Year and having spent a lot of time in and out of hospital. She did not sit her Leaving Certificate but had already taken the first baby steps in a career in the public service. "In 5th Year I began a course called Vocational Preparation & Training. During this course we went into the workplace for six week's work experience where my determination really began to shine. "

When she realised that the school authorities were intent on placing her in sheltered employment, she immediately let one of her teachers know that she was not happy with this. "So Miss Clerkin wrote to the Senior Staff Officer, Niall Mc Donnell at Wexford Co Council who wrote back to say that he would be glad to have me do my work experience there." Reck was placed in the Finance Department and after those initial six weeks was asked back on a number of occasions before eventually being offered a pemanent position with what was then Wexford Corporation. "I was glad I was successful not just for myself but because I also wanted to set an example for other students facing similar hurdles or attitudes."

In May 1987 she started work as a full-time employee with Wexford Corporation working as a receptionist/telephonist, a position she held for almost twenty years before transferring to Wexford Co Council. She was also getting more involved in sport and with the Spina Bifida and Hydro-cephalus Association Ireland but her everyday ambitions were the same as any other young woman.

"It used to be the normal things like getting married, my dad walking beside as I wheel up the aisle, having kids and things like that. Now those things haven't happened. In my twenties I used to get upset about that and there was no one really I could confide in. People say that if you acquire a disability it's worse than being born with a disability. I don't necessarily agree with that argument. I do miss not having children, getting married and all the normal things. Sometimes people would tell me that what you never had, you never miss and I sometimes shout in my own mind 'how would they know?'"

But Edel Reck got on with living. Just as she never had much faith in a 'miracle' from the early visits to Lourdes, she equally didn't believe that life – or anyone in this world or anywhere else – owed her anything. "I never felt that. As I got older my friends would be going to nightclubs and I would only occasionally be invited along. Sure I was upset then as I wanted to go too but I just got on with it. I got involved with other things, got other hobbies and kept pushing myself. Travel became my going out."

Her parents had been among the founding members of the Wexford branch of the then Irish Association for Spina Bifida & Hydrocephalus in 1970 but when Edel reached her late teens they stepped back for her to become more involved. In 1994 she became the National Youth Officer. "I was a voice for the members essentially and I would raise any of their concerns at national level. I suppose I would have been well known around Wexford and my parents would have been very active when I was young so that's how I was asked to take up the position first in the local branch which I held for many years".

Then at the end of the decade, it all changed. In May 1989 Reck's plane touched down at JFK airport in New York. She was in America to compete in the New York State Games, having brought together a national squad. The trip came about when the Executive Director of the New York State Games, Susan Gordon Ryan, invited the Mayor of Wexford, Alderman Dominic Kiernan to assemble an Irish team to compete at the event. So he asked Reck if she could help. The 19-

year-old knew nothing about fund-raising but learned the ropes, got the team organised and got ready for America. I wasn't the world's greatest athlete but I had already competed in a number of track and field events including the discus, shot putt and javelin. But that trip to New York was significant for reasons other than sporting."

Bewitched by the Big Apple, Reck experienced Gotham as a place where her television dreams were true. It was big, brash and busy: colourful with cars larger than houses and a skyline that traced out her wildest expectations. This was another planet, a new world, and even though she couldn't have known it then, it marked the beginning of a new phase of her life. Up to then there had been a few trips across the Irish Sea, a number of visits to Lourdes and a handful of sun holidays in Spain. Confinement was in the mind, she said and after New York there would be no stopping her.

"Apart from those few family visits to Lourdes it was my first time outside of Ireland and arriving in a country where the buildings touched the sky and the cars were big as houses stoked my imagination and fired sense of adventure. Right there and then I was bitten by the travel bug. After Manhattan there would be no looking back."

In 1990 and again in 1991 she returned to New York and to the State Games. That same year also saw the beginning of another passion, travelling to major track and field events. The World Championships in Tokyo was the first sticker on her travel bag. It was there that Reck first ran into Roger Black, the British sprinter who anchored Britain to gold in the 4 x 100 metres relay despite losing his shoe on the final bend. But even that dramatic episode could not have prepared him for the Irish woman in the wheelchair who crashed into him accidentally on purpose at the city's Narita Airport. "He bought me coffee, we had a chat and have kept in contact ever since. We still laugh about that first encounter to this day."

The former Olympian has fond memories of those days when Edel Reck travelled the world to see the best in action. "During my athletic career Edel was one of the most loyal followers of the team," he says. "I remember meeting her in 1991 in Tokyo – a successful year for me as I won gold and silver at the World Championships. My first impression was that she was both passionate and knowledgeable about athletics. Edel is clearly a determined person who doesn't let obstacles get in her way- she spent a lot of time and money travelling to support us and despite her many setbacks over the years she continues to inspire and educate others."

Black now works as a motivational speaker and TV presenter but regards Edel Reck as one of the most inspirational people he has met throughout his career. "Edels belief that 'nothing is impossible if you put your mind to it' is one that she puts into practice every day. She has not allowed her physical disability prevent her from living a full and exciting life. She is a very special lady."

Following major surgery in 1993 Reck was out of action for a year. But that operation gave her a new lease of life. "Without it I may not have seen so many exciting places and done so many exciting things," she says. "Every day I think of the lovely doctor, Dr Tom Lynch, who performed that surgery."

Her next big sports trip was to the World Championship in Gothenburg in 1995 where Sonia O'Sullivan won gold in the 5,000m. The Cork athlete did not have a flag but Edel Reck's tricolour saved the day. "I was going crazy in the stand when Sonia won and a press photographer ran over to me and asked me for my Irish flag because Sonia did not have one. So Sonia was carrying my flag for all those press photographs that went around the world."

Five years later, there was another emotional moment when O'Sullivan won silver in the 5000m at the Sydney Olympics in 2000. "During the presentation ceremony the tears were rolling down my face as the Irish anthem was being played. A couple of stewards and some spectators came over to me and helped me stand up for the national anthem. That was really nice and I'll never forget it."

Over the years Reck has been a familiar face at major athletic events – World and European championships, as well as the Olympics – and has met some very famous faces. "I met Carl Lewis who had spotted me from going to all the athletic meetings. He just

PHOTO MARK SHEARMAN

came over and said 'hello' and started chatting to me. He gave me a signed tee-shirt. Linford Christie gave me a signed singlet and I met Michael Johnson at the World Championships in Athens in 1997 where he gave me his gold shoes. He just walked over and said, 'would you care to have these mam?'

In 1994, she was elected as National Youth Officer with the Association, a year-long post that was extended to three when she was re-elected by members. She wanted to make her mark and do something special: an adventure trip for the young members that they would never forget. "At first I thought about the Irish training ship, *The Asgard*, and I rang the Department of the Marine. They told me about the *Lord Nelson* which I had never heard of before. So I contacted them, got the information and sent it to the different branches around the country and told them what I was planning. At the National Executive meeting I had all the details and all the research done and after some discussion it was decided to give it a go."

There were two *Lord Nelson* trips. The first was in December 1996 and the second in February 1997. There was also a TV documentary made called *Against The Wind*, shot during the second voyage. "I just got this mad notion into my head and wrote to the then Head of Features in RTÉ, Mick McCarthy. More or less immediately he came back with a positive response. He told me that he would get me a transmission slot for the documentary and told me also to contact an independent production company. I spoke with Gerald Heffernan at Frontier Films as I didn't know of many others at that time and I set about helping to raise the funds to make that documentary."

In 2001, she was re-elected as the National Youth Officer and organised a skiing trip to Loon Mountain for one of the Association members, Shane McDonagh. "One afternoon I suggested to a journalist friend that he should try skiing using the same equipment as me. After that my imagination started running away with me. I thought how good it would be if people with mixed abilities could partake in similar adventure activities with a celebrity companion. Not only would it make great TV but it could help make a difference whilst accomplishing something new and having fun at the same time."

There was also paragliding, hang-gliding, whitewater rafting in the Grand Canyon and in Peru, hot air ballooning over the Andes, horse-riding in the Mojave Desert, sailing in the Caribbean and safari in Kruger National Park. "I do those things for the excitement, the thrill and the fun and also the challenge, to see how I'll get on. Being in the outdoors makes me feel alive and free. My biggest challenge? I reckon that is the *Lord Nelson* between the whole organisation of the trips and then the challenge of being on the boat for days. It was tough going. Also being on a bi-ski. That was scary and exciting at the same time. I had never skiied before. But I don't get fazed too much. I will try everything."

In 1995, she visited Peru, where apart from white-water rafting and hot air ballooning, the highlight, and her toughest ever physical challenge, was climbing to the top of Machu Picchu. "According to the company I travelled with I was the first wheelchair person in their history to get to the top of Machu Picchu on my own steam but I don't know if that is still the case. There were two other wheelchair users on that trip but they were lifted up all the steps through the ruins. I wanted to do it by myself so I got out of my chair. The people who were assisting me lifted my chair and I dragged myself up on my well cushioned bum! I went up backwards, over thousands of steps. It took me nine hours to get up and down. It was very emotional when I got to the top. I cried then: a combination of pain, excitement, fulfilment."

After Peru, her travelling was put on hold when she had to undergo two long rehabilitation periods in hospital. Firstly, in 2008, when she broke her two ankles and was confined to bed for six months, and in 2009 when she was hospitalised for eight months due to a broken leg. But Edel Reck still dreams on of other adventures and far horizons: of places that she has not yet seen and epic treks yet to be undertaken. "I'd love to go around the world by wheelchair. Doing it by road, rail, boat, whatever and overcome the various challenges en route. Maybe I could do it as a relay event, involving other wheelchair users or visually impaired/deaf or whatever as well. And I'd love to go mountain climbing some day as well."

Back in the early days, when Edel Reck first contemplated putting her own story into print, we toyed with a number of possible titles. What about 'Against the Odds'? No! Perhaps something like 'The Impossible Dream'? Finding a title was proving difficult. Edel Reck knew that whatever was on the cover of her book would also frame her character and herself. The notion of the book's title reflecting her in a heroic light didn't sit easily on her shoulders. Edel Reck's argument is that adventure holidays for people with physical disability should be the norm rather than the exception.

So rather than pen her own story, she was hoping for a sort of travel guide for those adventurers with a physical disability. Of course that is Edel Reck: a trailblazer who has skiied the Rockies, jumped out of an airplane at 12,000 feet, climbed Macchu Picchu and negotiated the rapids of the Colorado river in a rubber boat.

Edel had the experience under her belt, the knowledge in her head and the fire in her soul. She had been there and done that better than most able-bodied people. Boundaries were only there to be crossed. "I like testing myself as much I can, people are only limited by their own imagination she says, a phrase that has become part of her philosophy.

It was impossible to write this as a pure and simple travel guide, just as *Two For the Road* is not a straight-forward TV travel show. Edel Reck's story as an inveterate traveller and committed adventure seeker intertwines with the advice and information like some sort of rogue strand of DNA. It's travel Jim but not as a lot of us know it.

For example, you're checking into a second-rate motel somewhere in the boondocks of New Hampshire. You're given a room key. The only problem is that it's for the second floor, up two flights of wooden stairs. In your wheelchair this is not going to happen. The receptionist apologises and relocates you to the ground floor. Now there's a door ledge to negotiate. Eventually a ramp is located. You're perplexed because when you rang from Ireland you were assured that your room would be wheelchair accessible. Even so you had to travel 3,000 miles to find out that you would need the arms of Arnold Schwarzenegger to safely get into your room.

Or maybe another time it's early morning and you're famished. But to get to the breakfast table you have to first leave the main building, wheel through the snow, and then find that the wheelchair accessible door is locked. After more than twenty years of adventure holidays in unlikely places Edel Reck has many such stories to relate: stories of too narrow doorways, too steep steps, unerringly rude staff or people who simply just don't see you. You gotta be there, she says to know what it's like. Don't believe the brochures or the PR spin.

Since Loon Mountain, Edel Reck's work with the Association has tapered off, punctured by a certain amount of disilusionment. "I think that the Association has come a long way in the last decade or so but it is still very much run by parents meaning that some people's voices get lost and are sometimes not

heard. I believe that the Association is very parent and child-orientated and there's not much there for the older members. In fact, people like me are a lot older than some of the parents. There's not much for us now, but I hope that this will change."

So she set about doing her own thing: travelling the world and germinating the idea for *Two For the Road*. As well as being a series of some-times unlikely adventure tales, the series is also the story of seeing life from the perspective of the wheelchair-user or the visually impaired or the person who is unable to walk unaided. "Even if it can help just one person it will have achieved what we set out to do," says Edel. "I hope that it will break down barriers and that it will show what people with a disability can achieve instead of just being dismissed as not being able."

While she does not believe that there has been a major shift in people's attitude towards those with a disability, she is hopeful that programmes like *Two For the Road* can help swing things in the right direction. "*Two For the Road* will hopefully help bring about change. So instead of people going around with their eyes wide shut, maybe they'll start to open them up. So, I hope that people will follow their dreams, but keep them real at the same time. Anything is possible if you can see it clearly in your head first. Keep trying, and don't ever give up, because life is full of endless possibilities. The only time you fail is when you stop trying."

Like that day on Loon Mountain.

CHAPTER TWO

Aine Lawlor and David Proud

Aine Lawlor

Aine Lawlor is a radio journalist with Ireland's state broadcaster, RTÉ. For sixteen years she has been a presenter on *Morning Ireland*, a daily current affairs show with the highest listenership in the land. She had never skied before – mainly because she has a morbid fear of heights.

David Proud

When he played Adam Best on *EastEnders*, David Proud, who was born with spina bifida, became the first ever disabled actor to portray a character with a disability on the BBC soap. A full-time actor and keen basketball player, the 28-year-old's long-term ambition was to ski. He too has a fear of heights.

33

The Location

Morzine is a small ski resort in South Eastern France, close to the Swiss border and a short hop from Geneva. Ski 2 Freedom, an independent non-profit organisation founded in 2007 by Catherine Cosby, organises ski classes, accommodation and tuition at the resort. Cosby, the mother of a profoundly disabled daughter, is the current director of Ski 2 Freedom which facilitates adaptive skiers at a number of European resorts where the specialist instructors are available. The organisation's motto is 'nothing is impossible' as it promotes snow sports and mountain activities for disabled, special needs and disadvantaged children and adults. Catherine Cosby was in Morzine to welcome David and Aine.

The Challenge

Sit-skiing is exactly what it says. Rather than standing on a pair of skis you are strapped into a moulded and padded seat just a couple of feet above the ground. The tandem ski, which is for those with very limited upper body strength, has a handle bar at the back which the instructor holds to control the direction. A mono-ski (single) and duo-ski (two skis) are for skiers with greater ability and can be used in conjunction with ski paddles or outriggers.

Aine and David started off in the tandem skis which allow very little movement. Both graduated to the bi-ski with David trying the mono ski, which has greater manoeuverability and the potential for higher speed. In both the latter cases you can use a pair of outriggers to guide yourself down the slope, carving left or right as required.

The Shoot

"There was no snow when we arrived in Morzine and we were worried," says Alan Gilsenan. With a limited budget the film crew revised their plans, deciding that they would have to go higher to find suitable conditions. But at the end of the second day the snows came: heavy and blizzard-like. In the waiting time Gilsenan discovered that both his would-be adventurers had a common fear. "David was in fact far more scared of heights than skiing," says Gilsenan. "But both he and Aine conquered that together; an unexpected challenge that had nothing to do with their physical ability."

For the shoot David and Aine wore fixed cameras, Alan Gilsenan shot from a tandem ski, some of the ski constructors were recruited to film the downhill sequences but most of the footage was shot by the cameraman, Richard Kendrick, an accomplished skier. Overall it was a time-consuming process as it took approximately forty minutes to get to the top of the run while the descent, which was filmed, lasted a mere fifteen minutes. "The thing is that once you're in the snow you're useless unless you can ski so once David got into his adaptive skis he was as free as I was," says Gilsenan. "So our disability on the snow was our ability or lack of ability to ski. An interesting flip-around"

Alan Gilsenan also tried the adaptive sit-ski. "Strapped in there your movement is very limited," he says. "There was a sense that I was stuck in this thing and there was also the feeling of how people looked at you. And you wanted to say, 'No, I'm not the disabled bloke, I'm just the director. I'm not really one of them.' That feeling was really disconcerting and in a way that's quite appalling."

But there was no attempt to impose an artificiality on the challenge by setting up the action sequences. Gilsenan just shot it as it happened – or some cases didn't happen. "In terms of experiencing each others lives, like Aine Lawlor trying out the sit skis, I didn't want to do anything artifical," he says. "I thought that might be patronising and gimmicky."

However, on the slopes absolute beginner, David Proud, impressed his instructors with his ability and his willingness to try just about anything. "According to the people at Ski 2 Freedom, David was one of best ever debutantes at adaptive skiing," says Gilsenan. "He just got it. He had a natural athleticism and balance that most people, able-bodied or disabled, would not have. He was exceptional. In a way that made Aine the person who was the disabled skier."

Aine's Story

WHEN WE MET IN MID-MORNING in RTÉ, Aine Lawlor's day was already nearly over. *Morning Ireland* had wrapped and she was having a quick smoke outside the canteen. It was the summer solstice and the middle of a hectic year for the news journalist: six months that included the coverage of Ireland's banking crisis, a general election and the visit of Queen Elizabeth II and US President, Barack Obama. But the year began so differently, and so scarily, in a small corner of South-Eastern France.

"I got an email last Autumn from Martin Mahon about this new TV series," she recalls. "Initially it was for dog sledding in early December in Norway. Unfortunately it clashed with the Budget so I had to say that while I thought it was a great idea – with my dad, Eamonn, in a wheelchair I'm familiar with disability – I was unable to do it. I thought that was the end of that."

It wasn't. Yellow Asylum Films came back with an alternative suggestion: skiing in France in January. Lawlor, a mother-of-four and, by her own admission, a bit of a scaredy cat as far as anything physically taxing is concerned, was now in a slight bind. "Because I had already said no I didn't want to say no again but skiing is some-

thing I would never do because of my fears. But because of dad I just felt I had to do it."

Not only had Lawlor never been on a winter ski holiday before – a somewhat sore point with her family – she also had an extreme fear of heights. "Skiing was something that I'd never thought I'd do because the idea of me on a mountain was never on because I'd need a ski-lift to get up there and I have a fear of heights. So I agreed and then I just didn't think about it anymore. I just probably hoped that it wouldn't happen. Then somehow it did."

Fear is not something you'd normally associate with this award-winning journalist who was the Students' Union President at her old alma mater, Trinity College, and who has over her broadcasting years struck fear into even the most battle-hardened politician. But when series' researcher Moira Lawson accompanied Aine Lawlor to the ski store to check out equipment ahead of the trip, she was in a daze. "I was just speechless with fear that day," she says. "I remember coming home with the ski gear and my daughter just laughing at me. I was thinking then, I can't do this. I will just ring them up and pull out."

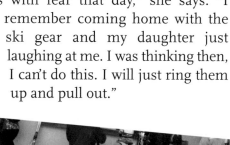

But the professional – and emotional – side of her prevailed. Not only did Lawlor think the TV series was a novel approach to understanding disability, but the image of her father was always at the back of her mind. "Because of Daddy I felt that I had to go to Morzine, especially as I know that using a wheelchair is such a different life," she says. "And no matter how much you care for someone who is in the wheelchair you still don't understand what it's like to be in there. *Two For the Road* seemed to me a new way of showing that and it wasn't just a celebrity thing. It was a real challenge as well.

Uncharacteristically Lawlor was very quiet the first day she arrived in Morzine. That Sunday night, when her instructor Françoise, measured her for the sit-skis it was a nerve-wracking experience. With each passing hour the fact that she would be skiing was becoming more real. She smoked a lot of cigarettes. She knew little about her travelling companion – apart from the information her daughter had gleaned from Google. But they immediately got on: especially' when they discovered they shared a fear of heights.

"I was really lucky to end up being partnered with David because he's incredibly sweet and bright. He's quiet but very determined and

sort of impish. He told me that he was afraid of heights too. I remember on the Monday when all the others were up the mountain doing the recce, we both sat on my balcony. As we sat there, looking at the ski slope, the pair of us more or less said: Oh holy God! Just look at the height of that! And they're telling us that we are to come down that?'"

"I didn't like the mountain when I saw it this morning. I watched people walking up to the lifts in all their ski gear and I couldn't believe that I was going to join them. It seemed like they came from another planet and it wasn't the planet I should be on."

(from Aine's Morzine diary)

Before heading out Lawlor popped a Xanax pill to steady her nerves. "There was no way I was going onto that ski lift without one," she says. Her ski instructor, who went by the name of Tiger, did his best to keep her calm and focussed. But on the steepest chair lift, the pulley stopped when they were half way up leaving them suspended in mid-air. "It must have been the tablet kicking in because I decided that I was just going to breathe, I was going to trust in Tiger and I was going to live," says Lawlor. "After that I wasn't thinking. I was just breathing. Then I began to see it as one of the most beautiful places I'd ever been."

"I watched the kids on the skis today, lines of them trailing down the slopes and they were so brave, the way kids are. I thought to myself how pathetic that a woman in her forties can't have as much courage as these guys."

(from Aine's Morzine diary)

That first day was a blur of fear and action and closed with a festival-like event as a local skier, who had triumphed in the Winter Olympics, had come home and was to be feted on the ski slopes. Aine and David skied down the course first – with some help from their instructors – and they were followed by the champion skier. But in her tandem-ski at the bottom of the run, and with a large crowd milling about, Aine was unable to fully see the action.

"I didn't want to ask the others because they were busy," she says. "That experience reminded me of my dad when he wants something but can't get it himself. Even to reach under the chair you need help from someone else. I had been aware of that with my dad but you don't know what it feels like until you are in that position. That time at the bottom of the ski run in Morzine was the first time I had that feeling and I was thinking how often Daddy must have the same feeling."

On the second day, Aine Lawlor was almost looking forward to the skiing. The fear had melted a bit and her fellow debutante skier was showing how the skiing could be mastered. "I was probably still as big a klutz as ever on the skis but I was beginning to enjoy myself," she says, as she went out on a bi-ski but the instructor always in close proximity. "I was able to enjoy the mountain. I

wouldn't have even got up on a motorbike before this but that lunchtime I got up on a skidoo with the guys. We went really fast and it was brilliant."

On both days she used the sit-ski – regular upright skiing is something she reckons she will never do – and was in admiration and sometimes awe of her colleague who took to the sport with an ease and enthusiasm. "David seemed to really good at tackling his fears. In any case he seemed to be more up for it than me. On the mountain he was fantastic. He got into the skiing so well and so quickly. He does sports as well so he's quite sporty."

After two days of adaptive skiing, the overwhelming emotion was one of relief. But also a sense of achievement marked by a special tribute from the instructors. "We came down the mountain when all the torches were lit and there was nobody else on the slopes. We all came down in this procession of swerves and whoops and skids and jumps! It was such a magic moment – to have the mountain to yourself in the darkness with all the lights and the snow. I never imagined myself being in that situation ever. It was incredible."

Being in someone else's shoes – or skis – gave her a new perspective on what it is like to be reliant on the kindness of others. "You can think of somebody else's issues or challenges or whatever but that's never the same as being in that situation. When you have to live and work within these limitations it's humbling in the best sense in that it gives you a humanity check. I don't think that my attitude changed because wheelchairs have been part of our lives for a long time. But it taught me to understand the feelings of frustration much better. It also changed me in that I don't want to be trapped by my own fears any more. That would be the biggest change."

Of course, her four children aged from 22 to 11 (or as she puts it, 'old enough to slag me') saw it somewhat differently. "They had a number of reactions and responses. The first one was 'why didn't you bring me?' The second one was 'are you now going to bring us skiing?' And then 'you didn't even stand up, what are you talking about', was the third."

But she felt that in her mid forties there was life still in her: a sense that life is not cut and dried and when someone emails you a crazy or even scary suggestion, maybe you should consider that adventure. "Yeah, it 's nice to know that you are not fossilising: that you can have adventures and do new things," she says. In a way it's more important as you get older and you think you know yourself that you push yourself outside your comfort zone. You need to go on reinventing yourself and changing yourself and doing things that you never thought you might."

Six months after Morzine, sitting in the RTÉ canteen, sipping coffee and eating a bacon sandwich, it all seems so long ago and far away and yet the emotional buzz is still close. The previous week she took her children to see a tall ship in Dublin port and as they skirted near the water's edge at the harbour wall, she didn't feel the usual fear. Something small but significant had changed.

A one-time frequent swimmer, she stopped following a bad experience. But this summer, with her kids, she went down a waterslide for the first time, and now she's planning to take swimming lessons again. "It's all about tiny steps," she says. After all she skied Morzine and lived to tell the tale.

"I remember when I came home to Dublin that first week in January. There had been very cold temperatures and the central heating was not working. So the house was freezing, the kids were cranky and the weather was dark and dreary. But I was on such a high that it has carried me though a lot of the year."

(from Aine's Morzine diary)

David's Story

"We had a light sprinkling during the night but not much. This prompted the crew to opt for Plan B. Plan A was not to venture too high up the mountain initially but with the lack of snow the crew headed higher up Le Pleney to find a better spot to film. The report from the top was good, snow and lots of it!"

(from David's Morzine diary)

DAVID PROUD was five years old when he left his home in Peterborough for an appointment at Ormond Street Hospital in London. It was only then that he was conclusively diagnosed with spina bifida. Up to that point, his parents, Tony and Wendy, knew that there was something wrong but did not know precisely what it was. "They were just dealing with the day-to-day of caring for a disabled child, trying to work out the walking and all that, they were learning as the went. It was a hard time for then."

In primary school he used plastic leg splints but as his condition deteriorated he began to use a wheelchair full-time in secondary school. Significantly his parents kept him in main stream education and he attended Sir Harry Smith Community College. "I think it's definitely better that you go through the mainstream because you aren't isolated in some way and it gets you ready for being in the working world when you're with a mixture of different people."

Growing up in Peterborough life was pretty much normal: at school he stood up to the bullies ("I was a bit of a geek") and his disability was just a part of his life. "For me I have always had a disability and didn't know anything different so it just seemed quite natural for me growing up," he says. "There were just some things in school that I couldn't participate in. I played football but I was in goal. So you stand there, freezing, and every ten minutes somebody will hit you with a ball. There are better places to be."

But it was on the school stage that he discovered his vocation. His very first role was Tiny Tim in *A Christmas Carol*. He was 13 and

got to act and sing. "Drama was always something I just liked to do, that notion of taking a role and making it your own a little bit," he says. "I just really like the challenge of that. If you can show something to your family and they can forget the fact that it is you and they get immersed in the story, then I like that."

He sang *Once* in *Royal David's City* a moment that had the audience in tears ("I don't know whether that was because my voice was so bad or otherwise") and he was happy. "There was a little bit of nerves beforehand but coming away from it when it has all gone well is a nice buzz. I never thought in a million years that I'd be doing what I'm doing now. I just felt at home doing it."

He continued acting in school, taking part in plays written by local playwrights and even writing his own GCSE piece in which he performed. "I did this scene in which I was upset and I purposely made myself tip out backwards out of my wheelchair," he says.

"Everyone jumped up out of their seat and went to help me! That was cool. I like playing with the audience." For his A Levels he was involved in a full production of *A Midsummer Night's Dream*. "I really love Shakespeare and there are parts out there that I'd like to play now. I think I might still be young enough to play Romeo depending on Juliet!"

Following school – he garnered nine GCSEs and two A Levels - he worked as a benefits administrator for the Department for Work and Pensions for four and a half years. "I was interested in a career in science but the course that I was going to do got cancelled because of lack of interest. So I decided to take a year out and reapply the following year to do a slightly different course. I ended up working for the government and didn't go to university ultimately. I just got into the routine of regular work. That was straight after A Levels. I got promoted quite quickly from a low clerical grade to decision maker level."

At the time he was playing in the Great Britain Wheelchair Basketball National League and his coach told him about an advert on the GBWBA website where they were looking for basketball players for a BBC show that was in development. Proud went to a number of auditions over two years before being cast as mixed-up teen, Charlie Johnson in *Desperadoes*. It was to be his first professional acting role – he took a three month sabbatical from work to play it – and when it was screened he signed his agent at the launch party. "It shows how little I know about this industry because the minute I signed I handed in my notice thinking that the next part was just around the corner."

If acting is a tough business, being a disabled actor is even tougher. "For disabled people the parts are rare at the moment but when they come up they are really good," he says. "Whereas able bodied actors will have two or three auditions a week, a disabled actor might get one a month. That's just the way it is."

To date Proud's film and TV work includes *Desperadoes*, BBC3's *Mischief*, a touching love scene opposite Billie Piper's hooker-with-a-heart-of-gold in *The Secret Diary of a Call Girl* and most recently the feature film, *NFA* (No Fixed Abode). But his best-known part remains that of Adam Best in *EastEnders*. "When people stop me in the street that's the part that they want to talk to me about," he says.

"Every now again someone recognises me from *Desperadoes* or *Secret Diary* or mistake me for the guy in *Glee*."

His old school, Sir Harry Smith Community College, also paid tribute to their illustrious past pupil by renaming the Supportive Skills Department the David Proud suite. "My mum actually works at the school and has done for years. They approached her with the idea of naming the suite after me. They sent me a letter. It was so touching that they wanted to do that."

In June 2010, Proud met Edel Reck at the Spina Bifida World Congress in Dublin. At that point he was considering another challenge – crossing Ireland on the back of a tricycle as a fundraiser for the Spina Bifida Association – when Reck proposed something completely different. "She gave me the brief outline of what was going to happen and I said 'of course, yeah'. I was going to try something that I'd never tried before ."

Proud's sport background would be an asset. His attitude was also a boon. "My thing is that if I haven't tried it before I'll have a go," he says. "It was also nice that I was going to meet somebody that I didn't know and go on this little journey with them. It wasn't until I actually got there and saw the chair lifts that take you up the mountain that I thought this could be scary. I hadn't thought about how we were going to get to the top of the mountain to ski. I thought that we might get a car to the top or something!"

The first morning in Morzine was a battle. Not only did he have to, even if temporarily, overcome his fear of heights but he also had to cope with the fear of losing his independence. "I'm very independent and any time I lose my independence I don't like it," he says. "But to get up that mountain you lose your independence because as a novice you don't know how to work the chair lift. You're just learning how to not fall over. So I felt like all the way up the mountain people were staring at me because I

was completely dependent on Françoise to get me up. But coming down the mountain I was in control of the sit ski and doing something quite cool. It all suddenly changed. Because you've got that independence back they are looking at you in a different light. They are looking at you in respect."

David Proud does not have handles on the back of his wheelchair for a reason. A speedy and dextrous wheelchair-user – he is a very useful basketball player after all – he doesn't like people to assume he wants to be pushed through the airport or the bus station or wherever: thus no handles. "I always aim for complete and total independence," he says. "Any time that my chair is taken away from me I feel odd and that's because someone is taking your independence away."

Once he was away from the chair lift, Proud was at home on the snow and on the skis. The first day he tried the standard sit-ski: a tandem-ski with a handle bar at the back that the instructors holds onto, unless they reckon you're good enough to go solo. "I thought that the instructor was still hanging on but because it's so well balanced, you don't notice," says David. "He just came skiing past me and said 'hello!' and I looked at him and felt like panicking but didn't. With him not aiding me I felt a greater sense of freedom and that felt amazing because I knew that I was in control. From then I just wanted to get better and go faster."

"Françoise my instructor taught me the basics whilst holding the back of my sit ski. I thought he still had hold of it but he then passed me on the left and waved! I was on my own. I have to say it was one of the greatest and most liberating experiences of my life. The sense of freedom was extraordinary."
(from David's Morzine diary)

He says his ability as a skier owes a lot to his experience in using a wheelchair. "When you push a wheelchair really fast along a pavement, it's like riding a bike – you feel every bump, every little difference in the pavement," he says. "If you're going really fast you have to anticipate what's ahead. So even when I'm talking to someone and wheeling along, I'll be scanning the path to make sure that I'm not going to hit something. So I think it's just the skill of sitting down and being able to feel the chair underneath you and react to it, the principle was exactly the same for the sit-ski. A lot of it is feeling the balance and trying to predict the snow in front of you and where you should turn."

The next day, having mastered the tandem-ski, he was ready to try the other options, including the bi-ski (a seat with, as the name suggests, two skis underneath) and finally the very fast, and slightly more tricky to control, mono-ski. Again he was a natural.

"Under the darkness of night, and on a mountain that had been closed for the evening, we were given the honour of being lead down the slopes with the ESF instructors holding flares. A moment I will never forget. "

(from David's Morzine diary)

David Proud was 28 when he visited Morzine. For the previous six years his life had been a hectic round of auditions and TV and film work. Some day he hopes to get married and raise a family. "In a way I've been almost married to my job these recent years," he says "You get little contracts here and there and you have to go. My job is like an episode of *Neighbours*: it's completely different from week

to week. Eventually it would be nice to settle down and maintain my career and have a family. I think that thirty is the ideal time."

He reckons that his fear of heights will probably never completely disappear. But his mantra now is: 'I've been skiing and it can't be as tough as skiing'. He concedes he'll always be a bit of a wimp but the man is being too modest. "People can overcome anything in life really," he says. "You just find a way to adapt. It's only when you take non disabled people and they are put into that world, you see how good the mechanisms are for disabled people to cope with their disability. I had to do that to overcome my disability."

Since his adventures in Morzine, David Proud has gone scuba diving for the first time. He continues to try new adventures but he plans to go back to the ski slopes this winter. "It's not so much opening people's eyes to disability, it's more opening their eyes to ability," he says of shows like *Two For the Road*. "It's about looking at someone and thinking, yes, they use a wheelchair but they're not just sitting in it. They are as agile in that wheelchair as I am on two feet. So it's opening people's eyes to ability and that everything in life can be overcome."

"Teaching sit-skiing is the instructors' job but empowering disabled people and helping them embrace life to its fullest is their passion. I will leave Morzine in the morning with happy memories and an eagerness to return as soon as possible: to visit friends and to continue to feel free, inspired and alive."

(from David's Morzine diary)

Epilogue

At the conclusion of the first adventure, during which all of the crew had to hurdle their own personal barriers, director Alan Gilsenan was realising that maybe this idea might just work as a TV series.

On the flight home he was confident. "I did feel that there was something there," he says. "What happened in that episode, and subsequent ones, is that the story became about the two people. The disability was there, but only in the background for most of the time. By going on an adventure, where two strangers meet up for a mad few days, they could actually learn about each other and also about disability."

CHAPTER THREE

Kamal Ibrahim and Edel Reck

Kamal Ibrahim

Kamal Ibrahim (25) is the current Mr. World. After seeing the action movie *Top Gun* at the age of eleven, he fell in love with flying and dreamed of becoming a jet-fighter pilot. But his love of adventure has taken him to many different places: from sky-diving in Florida to sitting in an adapted mountain bike on a hill in Colorado.

Edel Reck

After more than eight years of having a dream – and peddling it from pillar to post – Edel Reck's ambition of making a TV series finally became a reality in 2011 with *Two For the Road*. One of her hopes for the show, in which she is both a participant and Associate Producer, is that everybody tries a new adventure. But in a lifetime of adventure – skiing, hiking, sky-diving – she herself had never tried mountain-biking. Until now.

The Location

High in the Rocky Mountains of Colorado, and five hours drive north of Denver, is the historic mining town of Crested Butte. Nearby is the resort of Mt Crested Butte and at its heart is the Adaptive Sports Center (ASC), a non-profit organisation that provides recreational activities for people with disabilities and their families. The director of the ASC is Christopher Hensley and the Center is staffed by a highly motivated and highly qualified team of professionals.

The ASC facilitates an activity programme for both winter and summer. In the winter time the programme includes skiing and tobogganing; in the summer months, one of the main outdoor pursuits is mountain biking, both on and off-road. Its popularity is not surprising but while the panoramic vistas can take your breath away, the paths can be steep and challenging.

Three hours drive from Crested Butte is Colorado National Monument (or 'Monument' as it is referred to locally). This dramatic area of high desert land is in Mesa County and located close by the city of Grand Junction. In summer time temperatures can reach 100 degrees Fahrenheit during the day (nights can be cold) and drinking water is not available. It has many biking trails.

The Challenge

Adaptive mountain biking is an extreme sport. There are three main types: downhill, road biking and off-road cycling. On the downhill biking you can use a 2-wheel or 4-wheel bike but the adrenaline rush is the same. On the road it is hand cycling where you power the specially adapted bike solely with your arms. In both cases the going can be tough but exhilarating.

The Shoot

Alan Gilsenan and his seasoned film crew, which included researcher/photographer Moira Lawson, lighting cameraman Richard Kendrick and sound recordist Kieran 'Kiwi' Horgan, were boldly going into new territory with *Two For the Road*. The six-part series was going to throw up unusual and unexpected challenges. Those challenges began before they even hit the Rockies.

"The first thing about that trip to Crested Butte, which is quite banal in some ways" says Alan Gilsenan, "is that the journey from Dublin to Crested Butte made me realise what your average person with a physical disability goes through. You pass people in wheel-

chairs in airports all the time without a second thought, not considering all those aspects of access that they go through every day. That really came home to me on that first trip. The whole experience was quite disconcerting and even slightly horrific."

For four days in October, 2010, Gilsenan and his team filmed Edel and Kamal as they camped and biked on the trails of National Monument and Rabbit Valley in Mesa County, Colorado. "There was a certain amount of nervousness that it would all go OK," says Gilsenan. "There was one moment when Edel and Kamal came down the hill on the bikes that was quite scary. There was a lot of dust, they were very close and I was thinking, 'Jesus, this is all going to end horribly wrong. They are going to plummet off the cliff.' It was great action but you're also thinking are they totally going to lose it!"

In Kamal and Edel, Gilsenan had two adventurers who were willing and usually able to try just about anything. But the emotion of putting yourself in someone else's shoes – Kamal used a wheelchair to get about and attempted to emulate Edel's daily routine – can sometimes be overwhelming. "I think Kamal suddenly realised in that moment he was trying to transfer from the bed to the chair, how tough this would be," says Gilsenan. "It was a very moving scene to shoot. In fact I think that little scene said everything that Edel was trying to say with this series. It was that thing of just for one moment the able-bodied person thinking, 'God if that was me now, how would I cope?'"

Kamal's Story

"I remember the first time they put me into the wheelchair. Initially it was fun and I was enjoying doing wheelies and showing off. Then they brought the braces which prevented me from using my legs and suddenly, and unexpectedly, I felt afraid and constricted. I sat in the wheelchair and moved forward about a foot and had to stop because it became all too real for me. I began to imagine then what it was like to be paralysed."

(from Kamal's Crested Butte Diary)

KAMAL IBRAHIM grew up with a love of adventure and flying. His bedroom walls were plastered with images of all types of aircraft – civilian, military, aerobatic – and every day he would practice on the computer flight simulator. "My dream, as far back as I can remember, was wanting to fly airplanes," he says. "I was eleven years old when I first saw *Top Gun*, my favourite movie of all time. I remember watching it, unable to take my eyes off the screen, and thinking 'that's what I want to do for the rest of my life.'"

Kamal was born in Limerick city in 1985 to a Nigerian father, Abdul, and Italian mother, Roma. "When I was still very young, a few months or so, the family went back to Nigeria. My father owned a chain of restaurants in the capital, Lagos, and that is where I went to school although we did go back and forth to Ireland a few times. In 1993 and 1994 the Nigerian economy went downhill, so in 1994 we came back to Limerick."

He attended JFK Primary School in Limerick followed by Ard Scoil Rís. His younger sister, Zeina, was, he states, the academic one. After she did well in the Leaving Certificate she completed a certificate in Equine Science and went on to do a degree in Business and Finance while lecturing part-time. "I was never the academic one," he says. "I used to cause a bit of trouble at school. Nothing major, just silly things. But I was recently invited back to my old school, Ard Scoil Rís, twice to talk to the Transition Year students."

Kamal enrolled in the Limerick Institute of Technology so that he could become an officer in the Royal Air Force (RAF) and ultimately a pilot. He briefly considered applying to the Irish Cadets but as this was such a small operation the likelihood of securing a place was less likely. And there was the small matter that their planes just weren't fast enough for him. "I wanted to fly Mach 2, 20,000 feet, Top Gun. But because of the war in Afghanistan the entry requirements changed. Up to then you could apply to the RAF if you were from any Commonwealth country and also Ireland. Now only British citizens could apply. That was Christmas 2004. I was in college and was devastated by the news."

He subsequently wrote to the British Ministry of Defence (MoD) who informed him that he could still apply but it would be difficult to gain a place. Intent on following his dream he left college and got a job with the locally-based computer company DELL. "I worked there for 18 months, saved up all my money and went to a flight school in Florida where I trained for a month for my licence, having studied for the previous two months."

He was 19 years old when he got his private pilot's license in Aviation Studies from Ormond Beach Aviation, Florida. He was also stony broke. So in May 2005 Ibrahim returned to Ireland where he attempted to continue training but due to a number of obstacles – inclement weather, scarcity of instructors and money – had to park his dream. A chance encounter at a fashion show – he was convinced by the organisers to step out of the audience and onto the catwalk – sent him down a different path. Following that impromptu modelling moment, he was signed by the Celia Holman Lee agency where he worked for the next five years.

But he also continued with his studies. "I went back to college where I got a CIPD certificate in Human Resource management training. I also worked as a recruitment consultant for two and a half years while I continued modelling. By December 2009 I had four years of modelling under my belt with the Celia Holman Lee Agency."

In 2009 his life took another unexpected twist. "I was asked to enter Mr. Ireland because of my modelling experience. I declined at first but then agreed. I came first in that competition. In March 2010, because I had won the Irish competition, I was asked to compete in the Mr. World Competition which was being held in Incheon in South Korea. "

It was seven months after Ibrahim had won the national title. Now he was stepping into a totally different league with competitors from seventy-four different countries vying for the top prize. "The competition wasn't so much a beauty pageant as a boot camp," he says. "They were looking for someone to represent the organisation and travel around the world with them." After seventeen days, during which he was judged in fitness, fashion and cooking, Ibrahim took the top prize. "Without a doubt that win has changed my life," he says. "Not just the amount of travelling that I have done, but the people that I have met and the opportunities that have come my way."

Rather than opening doors for him, Kamal prefers to describe his win as showing him where the doors were. Since becoming Mr. World he has travelled the globe, worked with children's charities and seen his profile rise. With his new found ambition of carving out a career as a TV presenter, he made a number of small screen appearances. Then *Two For the Road* came knocking. With its combination of adventure and TV, it was tailor made for the man from Limerick. The show's concept was appealing from the outset.

"I thought the notion of experiencing life as a physically disabled person would be intriguing," he says. "I saw it as a challenge and also a learning experience. I wondered whether I could cope or function without the use of my legs. It was going to be a physical experience and emotionally honest. I like that because I'm not the kind of person who would pretend to be anyone or anything else. I liked the idea that it would be raw and honest and physical: capturing the essence of what I would be going through. That excited me."

Prior to *Two For the Road*, Kamal knew very few people with a physical disability. His cousin had survived a car accident but through his ambassadorial role as Mr. World and the Variety Club he is increasingly working with disabled and disadvantaged children throughout the world. With *Two For the Road* he was keen to be thrown in at the deep end: an attitude fostered and honed by years of adventure and extreme sport.

"I'm an adrenaline junkie," he says. "I had played all sports as a youngster – rugby, soccer, basketball, GAA. But while I swam competitively for eight years, I never really got into those other sports at school. What I really enjoyed was the high rush sports like sky-diving or mountain-biking or whitewater rafting or bungee jumping. That's my idea of a good, exciting sport."

Even so adaptive mountain biking would be an utterly new experience. And the first time he met Edel Reck and the staff at the Adaptive Sports Center in Crested Butte, he knew that here was something completely different. Accompanying Edel and Kamal on their four day adventure would be ASC staff members, Jacob and Cara. In his diary Kamal writes of this special duo.

"There was Jacob, the extremely mature and professional 26-year-old who was very knowledgeable about a lot of what Crested Butte had to offer. There was Cara, an attractive young girl who, as it happened, was completely deaf and wore a special device so she could hear us. I knew after meeting everyone that the next few days were going to be great – and I wasn't wrong."

The team – ASC staff, film crew and Edel and Kamal – drove by mini-bus to National Monument which was to become their home for the next three days. "We camped in Rabbit Valley," says Kamal. "That was special, being out there under the stars, sitting by the camp fire, doing wheelies in the chair. It was fun without the braces but with the braces it was not that funny. The moun-

tain biking was so competitive, hurtling down the hill in this amazing countryside. It was a blast."

There were two days of biking. The first was road-biking: difficult to maintain your balance but not particularly taxing. Initially Kamal had problems with stability but once he mastered the correct body position it was relatively plain sailing. "Of course Edel had no problem with that," he says. "Once we set off, we were in a race and Edel is very competitive: she wanted to win. She said from the beginning, 'Don't go easy on me' and when she said that, I knew that she meant it. I didn't have to be anything else apart from myself when I was around her."

To replicate Edel's physical situation, Kamal's legs were restricted by specially designed braces. In his diary he wrote of the experience of using a wheelchair for the first time and also the physical and

psychological impact of the braces. "With the braces on I could not walk and it felt very real for me then," he says. "I had to ask for help for everything from moving bags to trying to get somewhere and I felt very ashamed and frustrated because of it. I did get upset but I held myself together. I really didn't like wearing the braces from then on."

"The bikes are designed for those who can use or feel their legs. It was very uncomfortable and from the waist down I felt very claustrophobic. I just wanted to stretch. My back was aching from the awkward positioning of the seat and I couldn't help but wonder how wheelchair users could use these bikes so easily. For an able-bodied person it was really a tough task."

(from Kamal's Crested Butte diary)

On the second morning Kamal had to effect a transfer from the wheelchair to his bed. It seemed a straightforward task. But it was to prove physically challenging and emotionally draining. "That morning, when Edel woke me up, I had the leg braces on and I was to transfer myself from the bed to the chair. She was telling me, 'Put your hands here and lift your bum up'. That was fine until I was

half-way between the bed and the chair and my arms got really tired. I was only doing this for less than two minutes. In that moment I felt embarrassed because I am a young, fit and strong guy. I kept asking myself, 'why can't I do this?'. That, coupled with my wanting to break free from the braces, made me upset."

In that moment Kamal realised how difficult even simple feats must been for his travelling companion. "It struck me that Edel does this all the time. Now here I was, out of breath, tired and only halfway there. That really upset me – I was frustrated and tired. I felt very put in my place, humbled even. It gave me then the real under-standing of what it is like to live with a physical disability. That, more than any other moment, stood out for me. In that moment I truly realised that there's nothing easy about being disabled. That might sound obvious but I didn't realise it until I was in that position."

"It's funny. I knew life was harder for someone using a wheelchair but still thought everything was made easier as a result. Well more than anything I've learnt that disabled people may have obvious restrictions but as a result develop other strengths – and often these are strengths we don't see."

(from Kamal's Crested Butte diary)

"So what did I learn? I learned how little I knew about what a disabled person's life is really like and what they go through each day. I also learned that people who are physically disabled have strengths in other areas, not just physical strengths but emotional strengths too. I learned that I will never be uncomfortable with someone who is disabled. I will never act differently with someone who is disabled. In a lot of ways these people are stronger than me."

A few months after his trip to Crested Butte, Kamal was on one of his trips as a Mr. World ambassador (to date he has helped raise over $3 million for children's charity). An encounter brought back memories and lessons learnt during his trip to the Rockies. "I met a family where both parents were blind and their two adopted children were blind as well," he says. "We said to them that if they ever needed anything to give us a call and the girl turned to us, thanked us and said: 'and if you ever need anything, give us a call'. Damn right, I thought. Just because someone is disabled, it doesn't mean that they are at a disadvantage."

Edel's Story

"In October 2010 I set off from my home in Wexford for Dublin Airport but I had to stop en route about three times to use the bathroom. I was feeling so nervous I just couldn't help it."

(from Edel's Crested Butte diary)

ALTHOUGH A LIFE-LONG ADVENTURER who had tried her hand at most extreme sports, Wexford woman Edel Reck had yet to attempt adaptive mountain biking. "I had met a lot of people who had done it when I was in Crested Butte skiing in the winter time," she says. "Many of the other adaptive skiers also did mountain biking and they were raving about it so I was just dying to try it. That was the challenge that I picked for myself as I had done the rest before."

Edel researched what lay ahead, investigating the difference between regular biking and adaptive biking and what it would physically mean to her. "The main difference for adaptive biking is that there is some adaptation to the bike depending on the physical disability. For example with the road biking I was using my hands, it was all hand propelled. With the down-hill it's gravity that takes you down the hill. You steer using handlebars. In both cases you're quite close to the ground."

Edel first met Kamal at Denver airport, having travelled from Dublin via London. Her nervousness at meeting her travelling companion was immediately dissipated by

Kamal's warmth and enthusiasm. "He got into the spirit of the adventure from the moment I met him," she says. "He was by my side throughout the whole trip and really put me at ease. We were stuck together like glue." From Gunnison, where they met by Cara and Jacob of the Adaptive Sports Centre, the party completed the final leg of their trip to Crested Butte.

Edel had been to Crested Butte and the Adaptive Sports Center a number of times before, having skied in their winter sports programme. "Crested Butte is an old mining town in the heart of the Rocky Mountains. The Adaptive Sports Center was set up to enable people with a disability to enjoy outdoor pursuits with their friends and family as equals. It is in the middle of Crested Butte Mountain Resort which is a regular ski and summer resort. Thousands of people pass through the Center year after year. It is a fantastic place and the people who run it are amazing."

The 'cast' and crew arrived in Crested Butte resort in the limbo between winter and summer season so most facilities were closed. In a way they virtually had the place to themselves. That night they had the luxury of a hotel and the following morning they set off by mini bus for the great outdoors, and great unknowns, of National Monument, deep in the heart of Mesa County. Here, in the high desert terrain, the days are hot, the nights are cold and drinking water is not available.

"For three nights we camped in National Monument," Edel wrote in her diary. "This setting was truly spectacular. Kamal helped me to pitch my tent and we had great craic and proceeded to have that same or even better craic over the coming days. Kamal liked his sleep and once he was asleep, he was dead to the world. One morning while the guys were filming I headed over to his tent to try and waken him. I could have thrown water over him but I decided to be nice. He jumped up and took it in good spirits."

Strapped into the mountain bike, Edel rediscovered just how competitive she could be. On the road climbs and on the downhill races, she didn't just want to participate, she wanted to win. In those moments caution was thrown to the wind. "I didn't realise I was such a big show-off," she says. "But it also confirmed to me that if I put my mind to something I'll do it. It's my old mantra, 'if you can dream it, you can achieve it.' Even so she nearly came a cropper on the very first day, racing downhill, at one moment finding herself on just two wheels.

"The road biking was very strenuous and physically demanding. I wasn't fit enough really. If I had known how tough it was going to be I'd have been in the gym morning, noon and night beforehand. But still it was very enjoyable. We were not really racing each other but we ended up acting the maggot. I don't know whether Kamal was being easy on me and letting me get ahead but I don't think he was. He was behind me all the time so I reckon I did a lot better than him!"

The other side of the adventure was pitching tents under the stars. Eddel had requested that the two travellers camp out: not just to test herself but to prove that people with a physical disability are well able to tough it out just like anybody else. "A lot of adventure travel companies are reluctant to take people with a physical disability because they say that they don't have the facilities for camping out or whatever. I wanted to show them that if people are willing to improvise it can be done."

Improvisation was certainly part of the three-day camp, where toilet facilities were basic and getting about was a challenge, but sleep came easy. "The camping was both very exciting and very difficult at the same time," says Edel. "The terrain was particularly difficult, especially for Kamal who was using a wheelchair for the first time. It was exciting and nice to sit around a campfire at night swapping stories and planning for the next day's action. We did not have a proper loo so we had to use an improvised model – a hole in the ground. We also had to wash with just a bowl of water."

On the first morning it was down to business.

"After breakfast I was asked to show Kamal how to manoeuvre a wheelchair and he did a fantastic job. I don't think he was prepared or thought about what that meant or how he would feel. Moira got braces for Kamal's legs so that his would be heavy and awkward to lift just like mine are. I was asked to show Kamal how to transfer from his wheelchair onto the bed and again he was not prepared for the realisation of how that would be if it were real."

(from Edel's Crested Butte diary)

For Edel Reck such obstacles have been part of her everyday routine for most of her life. "People don't realise the physical effort it takes to get from A to B," she says. "In my own case I try to be in work every day for 8.30. To do that I have to be up at 6.30 having a shower. So it takes me two hours every morning just to get ready for work. In the shower it's especially difficult because you're wet and you're slipping all over the place. I can get in and out of the car in a minute or less as I have mastered that and am very used to it. But things like getting dressed or undressed also takes a lot of effort when you can't stand up. It's things like that that people wouldn't think about."

If climbing Machu Picchu is at the top of Edel Reck's toughness list, biking in Mesa County, Colorado, comes a close second. But the next time she's on a bike in the Rockies, she's adamant that she will be better prepared. "Going on an adventure like this requires you to be fit," she says. "Going unprepared is like going to Disneyworld and forgetting to bring the children! It gets very cold at night too so be prepared and wear lots of layers. I found this particularly difficult because my body can't regulate heat very well as my circulation is quite poor. This can be dangerous too, especially for anyone with paralysis."

Following their three day sojourn in the wilderness of Monument, the tents, bikes, chairs and equipment were packed up for the journey back to Crested Butte and 'civilisation'. That night there was dinner with the ASC people where tales were swapped and memories recalled. "Throughout our time together a song kept playing in my head: 'Stuck Like Glue' by Sugarland because that's exactly how we were," says Edel of her time with Kamal. The next day Kamal flew south to Florida where he was booked to do a charity event for the Variety Club. At Gunnison the *Two For the Road* team parted company. In her diary, Edel Reck wrote of the emotion of leaving Crested Butte.

"Going home for me was very difficult. I got on well with the crew and
Kamal and felt lonely knowing that it was all over." But she carried with
her a sense of achievement, having ticked yet another box in her list of
adventures. "It was physically very tough and I hadn't done it before so I
was relieved about that and also relieved that the two of us got on so
well. I feel very lucky and priviledged to have this life. I have always had
an attitude of gratitude. Gratitude for the family I have, my few good
friends and for having the ability to create new and exciting
opportunities for myself which in turn I hope will help others too."

CHAPTER FOUR

Sharon Shannon and Niall McDonnell

Sharon Shannon

Sharon Shannon was born in County Clare. In her early teens her love of horses suggested a career in show jumping but her natural talent as a traditional musician (fiddle and accordion) decided her destiny. Once of Ireland's best-known, and best-loved, musicians she has always nurtured a love of the outdoors and animals, especially dogs. In Norway she was going to experience both like never before.

Niall McDonnell

In August 1992, Niall McDonnell (then 22) was riding his motorbike through the village of Saggart in County Dublin when his life changed. A car smashed into him and he was trapped beneath the vehicle. As a result of that accident he was diagnosed T4 – paralysed from the mid chest down – and has lived his life since as a wheelchair user. "The pint glass is always half full," he says: a man who was born for the can-do philosophy that defines *Two For the Road*.

Location

Villmark Lodge, Norway, is perched on the border with Sweden, a remote outpost 220 kilometres north east of Oslo. The nearest community is the tiny hamlet of Ljordalen (population 300) and the region is famously cold, due to its inland location. During the winter months, snow is guaranteed and it is recorded that the great polar explorer, Roald Amundsen, famously trained his dogs here in advance of his expeditions. Today many other adventurers explore the vast and beautiful terrain of nearby Fulufjell National Park. The Lodge, which is run by Frank Nöllert, caters for a wide variety of summer and winter activities. *Two For the Road* arrived there in the heart of winter on December 2, 2010, when daylight lasts for just over five hours but the sledding is superb.

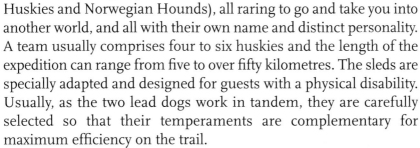

The Challenge

Villmark Husky Farm is home to over 150 dogs (Alaskan Huskies and Norwegian Hounds), all raring to go and take you into another world, and all with their own name and distinct personality. A team usually comprises four to six huskies and the length of the expedition can range from five to over fifty kilometres. The sleds are specially adapted and designed for guests with a physical disability. Usually, as the two lead dogs work in tandem, they are carefully selected so that their temperaments are complementary for maximum efficiency on the trail.

The Shoot

At Villmark Lodge in December 2010 the temperature was so cold that the film crew's battery packs drained and frostbite was a real threat. But there were challenges long before the film-makers arrived in the frozen north. In a blizzard-bound Dublin Alan Gilsenan was struggling to get out of his own home in the Wicklow hills.

He considered walking to the local train station, some half dozen miles distant. "It was quite bizarre," he recalls. "We left Dublin in the midst of a really cold spell with heavy snow and freezing temperatures. It was nigh impassable where I lived in Wicklow and any time I did get out it was very slow progress. On the day I flew to Norway I actually considered walking to the nearest train station, taking only as much as I could carry. Eventually I got a lift to the airport from our sound recordist, Kieran 'Kiwi' Horgan, in his four wheel drive. So we arrived in Oslo where the temperature was minus 20 and at Villmark it was minus 30 degrees. I remember stepping out into the car park and the cold hit me. That was an unbelievable experience. It was shockingly cold."

Such extreme temperatures presented technical problems for the filmmakers. "At those temperatures batteries don't replenish," says Gilsenan. "So a whole set of batteries were gone by the second day but we had brought back-up. We also kept them warm by stuffing them inside our jackets. There was also simple things like operating sound gear and the cameras. Our soundman Kieran got mild frostbite from operating the mixer. But against that it was a stunningly

beautiful place, really gorgeous. The actual filming was quite perilous at times because it was incredible how fast the dogs could go. We were on skidoos filming at full pelt and trying our best to keep up with them."

Niall and Sharon got on like the proverbial house on fire. "Niall was a happy-go-lucky bloke who had a motorbike accident but was driven by his desire to be the bloke that he was before," says Gilsenan. "And he seems to have succeeded in doing that. In fact he was so independent that sometimes you forgot that he needed a hand wheeling through the snow. The dog sledding gave him a sense of freedom because in the sled your legs didn't matter because you didn't have to use them for the run. Sharon really took to the skiing. The people at Villmark were very impressed with her because she was so natural at the dog sledding."

Sharon's Story

"At take-off, all of a sudden you go from the huge noise of one hundred and fifty dogs howling with excitement to a beautiful silence – hearing nothing but the sound of the dogs' paws on the snow. There was a bit of dodging of low branches. It was even more difficult for Niall in front of me to dodge them because they were very low. But he was doing a brilliant job. I began to doubt whether I'd manage as well as he did when it came to my turn in his adaptive sled."

(from Sharon Shannon's Villmark diary)

HARON SHANNON, modest and unassuming, jokes about how she ended up in a dog sled in Scandinavia being filmed for a TV series. "Maybe they had a big load of people on their list who couldn't do it so they crossed them off and then they eventually got to me," she says and laughs. "So I said yes!" She laughs again then, but this adventure was tailor made for someone like Shannon with a love of dogs. Her home at Salthill in Galway is a menagerie of four-legged companions with, at the latest count, four dogs and three cats in residence. She is also patron of the Connemara-based dog adoption and rescue organisation, Madra.

"I absolutely adore animals, especially dogs," she says. "So I was honoured to be asked to do something like that in the first place. But after that I really didn't know what to expect. In fact I didn't know whether I'd enjoy it or not but I decided that I would take a chance and do it – why not." So together with her manager, John Dunford (who is also a sailor, cyclist and all-round adventurer), they sallied forth for the outer limits of Norway where she found herself at the edge of the

Arctic Circle, at minus 35 degrees and facing a TV camera without her trusty accordion. It was a long way from here to Clare.

Sharon Shannon was born in rural Corofin (or Ruan, as both places claim her and her allegiance is divided). In the early years she "hadn't a clue" what she would do in life. "I grew up on a farm and my father used to breed horses as a hobby," she says. "He loves animals like I do. He had some Connemara pony mares which he used to breed with thoroughbred horses. The foals we trained for showjumping and they were fantastic jumpers. I loved working with the horses. It was something that I would have loved to have pursued but the music took over. The horses were a very expensive past time. I left home at sixteen and at that age you can't ride a pony anymore; it has to be a horse. So with me leaving home, and being sixteen and all the gigs I was doing, the music completely took over. But I'm still really passionate about the horses."

Her shyness – on stage Shannon is a different person - is countered by her passion for life and an innate kindness. Shooting *Two For the Road*, stirred memories from childhood when she was a special companion to a classmate. "In National School, there was a little girl who was a couple of years younger than me who was completely wheelchair bound," she says. "Her legs and her arms didn't work. I didn't know what was wrong with her but she was a gorgeous girl and I was mad about her. It was my job to look after her. I used to bring her here and there and everywhere. In a way I was like her in-school mammy. One of the teachers in the school just asked me to mind her. Maybe they knew that I liked her. She was great fun."

A founding member of the band Arcady, she later toured the world with The Waterboys and her 1991 debut solo album, *Sharon Shannon*, was one of Ireland's biggest ever selling Irish music releases. Throughout her career her musical influences have been eclectic, ranging from the reggae vibe on her 1994 album, *Out the Gap*, to hip hop single, '*What You Make It (da,da,da,da)*'. The classical violinist Nigel Kennedy asked her to join him on a tour of his 'Jimi Hendrix Suite', and she recorded *The Galway Girl* with Steve Earle.

The illustrious gallery of musicians that Sharon Shannon has recorded and toured with include Jackson Browne, Kirsty McColl,

John Prine, Christy Moore, Belinda Carlisle, Bono, Willie Nelson, Mark Knopfler and Sinéad O'Connor. She has played for US Presidents Bill Clinton and Barack Obama as well as the Irish Presidents, Mary Robinson and Mary McAleese. She is not only a performer but a composer and producer and owns her own record label, The Daisy Label. She made a cameo appearance (and performance) in the Neil Jordan film, *Ondine,* and her album, *The Galway Girl*, went more than four times platinum in Ireland. In 2009, at the age of forty, she became the youngest ever recipient of a Lifetime Achievement at the Meteor awards in Dublin.

Throughout her career Sharon Shannon has featured in many TV shows, including a special tribute to her on the top-rating Irish talkshow, *The Late Late Show*. But *Two For the Road* was something completely different. This presented another side to Sharon Shannon – without her trademark accordion or music – and she herself was aware of moving out of her usual comfort zone. "I was very nervous about the cameras and I was not sure whether I'd be self-conscious or not," she says. "But while I was nervous initially it didn't take long to get used to the cameras being there and to forget about them."

It helped that her travelling companion, Niall McDonnell, was as she puts it, 'a dote'. "Everybody loved him," she says. "He's really

down-to-earth and so easy to get on with. I know that one aspect of the programme was to see the world from Niall's perspective, that is to imagine myself in his shoes but I was thinking to myself: 'you're no good Niall, you're not complaining enough!'. To find out his difficulties I looked it all up afterwards when I got home. He's so positive and amazing."

At Villmark Lodge, Sharon immediately – and not unsurprisingly – bonded with the dogs, some of whom were actually taller than the musician when they stood on their hind legs to greet her. Initially anxious for the animals' welfare – when not working they have to be chained up in huts near the lodge – her fears were dissipated by the care and affection afforded them by their owners and handlers. "I really loved the dogs and couldn't stop thinking about them for months afterwards," she says. "I felt sorry for them as well because it upset me to see them chained up. But otherwise they were very well looked after."

She says that she's not a sporty person but walking her dogs at home – a daily duty that can take up to three hours – is enough to keep anyone on their toes. "I like being outside in the fresh air and I love nature and the outdoors," she says. "I also love swimming in the sea in the summer." She

is also prepared to try anything once, like a parachute jump in Australia or a bungee adventure in New Zealand. 'Mad things' she calls then and usually they are spur-of-the-moment decisions. "We were on tour in Australia and just happened to be in Byron Bay when we saw the fliers about the parachute jump," she says. "A year later I did a bungee jump in New Zealand which was much scarier than the parachute jump because you can see the ground coming at you at a massive rate. Very scary but I wanted to go and do it again immediately because it was such a rush."

Norway was different. For one thing she was unprepared for the shock of the cold. "It was absolutely freezing and the first day I wasn't properly prepared," she says. "You can put on these gels to warm you up but I didn't do that so my hands and feet were absolutely blocks of ice that first day. I was better prepared the next morning with those heat gels all over my body. They worked amazingly well."

But once she was out on the sled, gliding thought a winter wonderland of snow frosted trees, the biting cold and the occasional snapping branch were all forgotten. "That first day out it felt like we were in the sled for ten or fifteen minutes so I was really surprised when they said that we were out for one hour," she says. "That's a good sign. It must have meant that I liked it. It was really serene gliding along the snow through spectacular Christmas postcard scenery." But that was Day One, when Sharon was not restricted in her movements and did not have to use a wheelchair. So she went out on a five kilometre run in a regular sled: a one hour journey seemed to zip by in a flurry of snow and fur and scenery. Day Two was going to be a whole lot tougher.

"The crew were delighted with me on the second day because I had two falls. It's not a bit dangerous though because you aren't going very fast, you don't have very far to fall and it's a very soft landing in the snow. Still I did my level best not to let the dogs get away and held on for dear life to the sled. It was a natural instinct because I'm used to falling off horses and if you don't hold onto the reins you might have to walk for ages after a smart horse who doesn't want to get caught. It would be a lot more difficult to run in the snow with half a ton of clothes on you."

(from Sharon Shannon's Villmark diary)

That second day presented a greater challenge because Sharon was swapping roles with Niall, using a wheelchair and the specially adapted sled. The effort of getting to her sled in a wheelchair, pushing through the snow and hoping not to fall, required brawn and dexterity. "I nearly toppled backwards so many times it was mad,"

she says. Then she had to get into the sled without the use of her legs – again a complicated task. But once in, there was a sense of freedom as the dogs took over, and all you had to do was holler out the commands and occasionally apply the brakes.

Long afterwards – when the buzz of the run had died and the noise of the dogs was a distant echo – Sharon Shannon pieced together her brief but brilliant experience of dog sledding and the significance of being in someone else's shoes. "I never thought that much before about how big a deal it is to do something as simple as leaving your house and getting into your car when you're using a wheelchair," she says. "Trying to get from the chair to the car and then into the car and then taking the chair into the car with you and out again. Niall did that every day and it was no big deal with him."

"Niall was really inspirational and he has a will of iron," she continues. "It really makes you appreciate what you have. I suppose a lot of people don't really appreciate what they have until it is gone. When I think about Niall now I realise how much we take for granted and how lucky we are to have the use of our legs. We all complain far too much about things that don't really matter. I loved Niall's outlook on life and learned a lot from him. He focuses on all the positive things in his life and not the negative stuff. A world full of Nialls would certainly be a much better place."

Niall's Story

"You could feel the frost forming inside your nose when you breathed in. You could feel the crystals and when you breathed out you could hear them cracking and melting: a very strange sensation indeed."

SOME YEARS AFTER the road accident that left him paralysed, Niall McDonnell spent a year living in Australia. By then he was well adjusted to life using a wheelchair – not just the physical challenges but also the psychological ones. But to his friends the novelty of 'having a go' in the chair was still a bit of fun: an opportunity to practice 'wheelies' and see how they would cope. One day, like many others before that, a colleague asked if he could borrow the chair for a while. "We were in a car park and I was in the jeep so I said 'yeah, no problem.' So he got into the chair and wheeled about the car-park. When he came back to me there was a real intense look in his eye. I asked him what was up and he said 'people really look at you in this thing'. I told him that I didn't notice any more. I suppose in the beginning I was very aware of other people and their reaction. If you're shy it does impact on you."

Niall McDonnell – gregarious and garrulous – is far from shy. He is, after all, the man who climbed to the top of a Wicklow hill in

his wheelchair to propose to his girlfriend, Kathryn. And then he was filmed as he popped the question. The Dubliner's lust for life is undimmed by his disability: if anything here is a man who's even more prepared to try anything – at least once. So when *Two For the Road* came calling, Niall was ready, willing and able. "I thought that it was an

amazing concept right from the start," he says. "It is such an unusual mix of things. It has ambulant people engaging with those with a physical disability, there are also physical challenges as well as dramatic scenery and drama. There are so many elements and there were so many ways that they could interact."

"Once I knew where I was going there was the initial excitement of 'wow, dog sledding in Norway' but then I began to think of the practicalities. The cold and the snow can pose many problems for chairs. For example if you put a metal knife into a freezer, which is at about minus fifteen or so, well then take it out after a while and put it in your hand, you'll get an idea of what my wheels were like in Norway. We were basically in an outdoor fridge and my hand was on the wheel all day. Now we did wear special gloves but the contact between the metal of my chair and my body was something I had to be very aware of. My legs for example could be touching the frame of the chair so you'd have that extreme cold transmitting to the body. If you were to hold that metal knife from the fridge your hand would stick to it."

Niall McDonnell was always interested in anything to do with cars (he recently refurbished an old Ford Mustang which he brought in from Australia). "When I hit my teens I wanted to be a mechanic which I achieved to some extent when I ended up working with my friend Trevor in his family's garage," he says. But in August 1992 his motorbike was hit by a car in the village of Saggart, south of Dublin, and all changed. He had to have steel rods inserted into his back and spent months in recovery at the National Rehabilitation Hospital (NRH) in Dún Laoghaire. "The first time I met the counselor I cried my eyes out," he says. But from the next meeting onwards pragmatism took over. "I may have not been very happy with my injury and the consequences but I accepted it and moved on."

Initially devastated – he had lived a very active outdoor life – McDonnell accepted his fate with a stoicism that defines his attitude to life. "I was just unlucky to have been hit," he says of the accident that left him needing the use of a wheelchair. "But I was also lucky to survive."

Five years later his life changed again when he met his wife-to-be, Kathryn Smith, through an online dating service. On February 1, 2008, following a whirlwind romance, Niall proposed to Kathryn on the RTÉ series, *Marry Me*. But it was no ordinary proposal. Following a Herculean effort – and much cloak and dagger work to keep the operation secret from Kathryn – Niall managed to scale a hill in County Wicklow where he popped the question while a lone piper serenaded the couple. Kathryn said yes and on 17 July 2009 they were wed.

Niall McDonnell had always been an active person. "Prior to my accident I would have done a lot of hill walking and shooting and outdoors type activities. All that became a lot more difficult after the accident. I do go for a lot of walks with my wife, Kathryn, probably not as often as she would like because during winter it gets more difficult because it's wet and the rain soaks right through you. Sports wise I still go shooting so I'm still quite outdoorsy that way."

Before Norway, he has no hesitation in naming his greatest physical – and emotional – achievement. "Climbing that mountain and getting engaged," he says and laughs. "Without a doubt that was physically the most demanding thing that I have ever done. There was no faking the cold that day, it was freezing. It was probably warmer in Norway."

But dog sledding was something entirely new. "I hadn't even dreamt of doing it," he says. "I had hunted with dogs before though. Quite often when you're out hunting you wouldn't shoot things, you'd allow the dog to work, get them to make that pheasant take off. It's a natural instinct for the dogs and it's amazing to see them do what they are bred to do. When you don't shoot at the bird that they have tracked and driven into the open they really do look at you as if you're some eejit."

The first day he met Sharon, he also met the huskies and checked out the sleds. "The dogs were all very excited to see us as they thought that they were about to go for a run," he says. "They were also very curious about my wheelchair but apart from being shy about it they all reacted well."

"Now Sharon is very shy which is surprising as you'd never expect that. For someone to get up in front of thousands of people and blow them away with her music and musicianship and presence is amazing. So she's in the public gaze and it's difficult to get away from that. When I'm out there in the wheelchair you'll get a lot of interest. Kids are very funny because they'll ask you about the wheelchair but there's an interaction between you and the public that anyone who is ambulant would not have or do not normally see."

Niall's own gloves were not suitable for the extremes of temperature so he bought a new pair. But he was still anxious that first day in the sled. "I was nervous of putting my hands in the snow during the run. On the second day,

Frank, the owner of the Lodge, signalled to me to get active in the sled and once I started doing that, working the sled in tandem with the dogs, the heat came into me. That was the secret. The more active you were, not surprisingly, the less likely you were to feel the cold. You could feel the frost forming inside your nose when you breathed in. You could feel the crystals and when you breathed out you could hear them cracking and melting: a very strange sensation indeed."

Niall used a specially adapted sled, that had been designed a few years earlier by a friend of Villmark Lodge's manager, Frank Nollert.

"I had my first chance to sit in the sled today also, it is very comfortable albeit difficult to get in and out of as it is so low. But it was no real problem as the staff helped greatly to get me in and out of it. When I was in the sled I felt very secure and comfortable. It is made from Carbon Fibre and is extremely light in weight."

(from Niall McDonnell's Villmark diary)

Balance was the biggest problem. Then there were the low-hanging branches. Once the anchor was lifted, and the brakes were off, the dogs went hell for leather. "I did get a good whack from a tree in the very beginning," he says. "When I set off, we were going downhill

and through a copse of trees. The dogs cut tight to a tree in the left and I cut even tighter and got whacked in the head. The camera was sent flying but I put it back on and pointed the dogs in the right direction. It woke me up."

Apart from the technique required there were more conventional problems like communicating with the dogs. Apparently 'mush' in a Dublin accent can be very different from the same command in a Norwegian accent, as Niall discovered. "A dog doesn't necessarily understand your accent," he says. "My dad had a dog that was brought in from Scotland.

This was a beautiful little Labrador. A Scottish friend was able to get the dog to sit and stay and obey all these commands. So my dad thought this was brilliant and he told the dog to 'sit' but the dog just looked at him. The problem was the accent. He didn't understand the Irish accent. So it was like that in Norway. All these different accents – and the Norwegian dogs had a bit of a problem picking up the Irish accent initially."

Prior to the run both Niall and Sharon dressed in thermal suits as protection against the cold. Then they set off. Anna, the instructor, in the vanguard followed by Niall and then Sharon at the tail. Niall recalls that first run in his diary. *"The start was pretty quick and I needed to have one of the handlers hold the dogs back as the start is downhill and it is difficult if you have not done it before. Also as I could not break as hard as the others it could be dangerous."*

That first run was five kilometres. No spills, some thrills, lots of fun. The next day the run was nine kilometres and at a faster pace. Sharon was now in the adaptive sled: closer to the ground she hit the deck a few times but nothing serious.

"The start was really exciting for Sharon as she is quite a bit lighter than me and the dogs took off like a rocket. The instructor, Xena, who had been running with the dogs to slow them a bit went flying and the last thing I saw was the back of Sharon's sled disappearing over the edge of the hill at top speed."

For a greenhorn sledder like McDonnell the most difficult part was getting in and out of sled. He also knew that by himself he would not have been able to set up the team of dogs for the run. Once they are out of the kennels and in harness, they are feverish with anticipation. "So you need a bit of power to hitch them up to the sled," he says. "But once you're into

the sled you just let the dogs go and off you go." And once the run was over there was still work to do as the dogs needed to be rewarded for their efforts and enthusiasm. Both Niall and Sharon helped feed their team; buckets of a soup-like food that consisted of meal and water and also salmon fish heads. The dogs can eat their way through sixteen tons of fish heads in two months.

Even for someone as active and positive as Niall, *Two For the Road*, made a difference. As with most people, age had made him more cautious: the far away hills might be greener but maybe it was just too much hassle to get there. "In a way I had stopped trying new things," he says. "When you're younger I believe you're always trying new things. I'm heading for the mid forties now and I'd stopped trying new things. So perhaps it was time to start trying things again. You suddenly realise 'hey, when I was younger every second day I was trying something new. Maybe it's time to start doing it again?'"

Since the adventure in Norway, Niall and Kathryn have bought two dogs: a pair of black Labradors called Abby and Archie. "I believe my trip influenced my decision," he says. He also hopes to return to Villmark Lodge and experience it all again anew with Kathryn. But he will carry his memories of that first trip with him forever. "That day I first met with Sharon and we went up to see all the dogs, that particular moment was special," he says. "The dogs didn't care whether I was in a wheelchair or that Sharon was a famous musician, they just wanted to meet us. We were going to go out and do a job together. We were going to go out and go sledding."

CHAPTER FIVE

Trevor Brennan and Eamonn Victory

Trevor Brennan

Trevor Brennan was one of the hard men of Irish rugby through the late 1990s and 2000s. The Leixlip-born player, plied his trade at club level, including local club Barnhall, with provincial side Leinster, and most rewardingly with French side, Stade Toulousain. He was capped for his country 13 times in a career that saw him bag two European Cup medals with Toulouse. Throughout he was regarded as one of the game's toughest players. But then he had never sailed on the *Lord Nelson*.

Eamonn Victory

At the age of 26, Meath man Eamonn Victory, had his right leg amputated above the knee. At the time he was married with a child and was saddled with a mortgage. He was fitted with a prosthetic limb but it didn't slow him down Today he owns and runs a supermarket in County Louth with his wife Sharon, and has been skiing, canoeing and to a few Meath matches. But he was always curious about testing himself on the high seas.

The Location

The *Lord Nelson*, which is owned and operated by the Jubilee Sailing Trust charity, was the world's first Class A tall ship purpose built to be crewed by people of all physical and sensory abilities. To this end it includes many special onboard features including signs in Braille, lifts between decks and a speaking compass. Vibrator pads are fitted to bunks to alert people with a hearing impairment in event of an emergency, below deck there are wide aisles and throughout there are low-level fittings.

During the summer months the *Lord Nelson* sails about the British isles but in the autumn it migrates to the warmer climes of the Mediterranean and the Canary Islands. Since her maiden voyage out of Southampton in October 1986, the *Lord Nelson* has taken over 24,000 people on voyages of which 10,000 were physically disabled and nearly 5,000 were wheelchair users. The *Lord Nelson*'s sister ship, the *Tenacious*, is similarly adapted.

The Challenge

Apart from the permanent crew of professional merchant seafarers (including master, first mate, bosun, chief engineer, medical purser and cook), the *Lord Nelson* is manned by a 'voyage crew' of forty. So all people who board the ship are crew. It doesn't matter whether you are a person with a prosthetic limb or an ex-international rugby player, on this tall ship everybody is literally and metaphorically in the same boat.

As soon as you come on board you are briefed by the captain, handed a life jacket and assigned to a watch. Your duties onboard are varied, from preparing dinner below deck to climbing aloft to scrubbing the decks to even sailing the ship. All able-bodied voyage crew members are buddied up with one who is physically disabled. Each learns from the other, just as each helps the other.

For five nights and six days at the beginning of February 2011 Trevor Brennan and Eamonn Victory were buddies for a return trip from Las Palmas to Las Palmas, Gran Canaria. It took them into uncharted waters, physically and sometimes emotionally.

The Shoot

"We were only twenty minutes out of port and already most people on board were very sick," says Alan Gilsenan, who was among the casualties. "This made it very difficult to film as both our cameraman, Richard, and soundman, Kieran, got sick and found it very tough to function."

Apart from the rigours inflicted by the open seas, the *Lord Nelson* episode of *Two For the Road* was unlike any other for Yellow Asylum Films. The fact that they were filming a documentary did not exclude them from their regular nautical duties. Each of them – Alan, Moira, Richard and Kieran – were crew and they too had to work their watches. "You feel really guilty if you don't pull your weight because you know that someone else will have to do those duties," says Alan. "So it was pretty exhausting because you're trying to do your four hour shift in the middle of the night and then you have to rise early to film. At the end of the shoot we were in rag order."

Fortunately the two mariners – Eamonn and Trevor – stuck to their task despite the conditions and being sick for most of the voyage. "Eamonn was really ill and had the added problem of getting around the boat on one leg," says Gilsenan. "The fact that he got through it meant a lot to him. There was a lovely bond between him and Trevor. There's a huge warmth to Trevor. Trevor's a smart boy with the emotional intelligence to deal with most situations. And we were glad to have him on the boat with his strength."

There was also the decision to include Trevor's jocose references to

Eamonn as 'the cripple' as a natural part of the documentary. "We thought about that," says Gilsenan. "The first day we got to Gran Canaria we arrived very late so we didn't get to meet Trevor until the next day at breakfast. Trevor came in and walks over to Eamon and says, 'Right lads, which of you is the cripple!' That was him setting out his stall and as Trevor say that's his way of cutting through all the awkward stuff. His attitude would be, 'well why wouldn't' I slag him?' Eamonn took it all very well. And he slagged Trevor back."

Trevor's Story

"How did I end up on the *Lord Nelson*?," asks Trevor Brennan.

"Jaysus I still don't know the answer to that myself. I suppose I was just contacted by Yellow Asylum Films and they listed the different challenges from dog sledding to horse riding to skiing. I just said: 'Listen, give me the most difficult one! I want something challenging. And in fairness to them, they did! I wish I hadn't said that. I spent three days either hanging over a toilet bowl or over the rails. I didn't realise the sea could be as rough as it was."

I N 2007 Trevor Brennan's autobiography, *Heart and Soul* (with Gerry Thornley), won the William Hill Irish Sports Book of the Year award. It chronicled a rollercoaster career that was punctuated with incident and triumph, including two Heineken Cup wins, before ending in controversy with a lifetime playing ban from the European Rugby Cup(ERC), later reduced to a five year suspension on appeal. It's an honest book,' he says. "Or as honest as I could be without being brought to court." A few weeks before the ERC decision in March 2007 Brennan had retired from the game but in his career he never given anything less than body and soul.

Now on *Two For the Road* he was facing another challenge. One of the first times we see Trevor Brennan on *Two For the Road* he's hanging over the rails of the *Lord Nelson* and quite unwell. By that stage his dream of a leisurely cruise on the Med were long dashed by the reality of big boy sailing. "I was thinking that we'd sailing past the Canaries with the sun shining and blue skies but it wasn't that at all," he says. "When you go to bed at night you literally had to tie yourself to a cable on the wall in case you rolled out of the bed. If the weather had been good we could have had a dip in the sea but we never got off the boat until we hit dry land."

Brennan, who at one stage worked as a milkman, played as a second row or flanker in career that took him from local Leixlip side, Barnhall, to Bective Rangers, St Mary's College RFC, Leinster and eventually Stade Toulousain. He was capped 13 times for Ireland between 1998 and 2001 and played in the 1999 Rugby World Cup. He transferred to Stade Toulousain in 2002 on a two year contract but ended up playing with the French side for five years, a period that included three consecutive European Cup Finals (Toulouse won in 2003 and 2005).

Following the death of his younger brother, Damien, in the 1990s, the 6 foot 5 inch lock nearly quit the game, but his father encouraged him to continue. In a 2010 RTÉ documentary, *This Sporting Life*, he spoke about how his brother's death spurred him on and he was playing the game not just for himself but for Damien.

The first morning Trevor met Eamonn, the burly rugby player cut straight to the chase. "I figured that there were two ways you could go about it," he says. "You could try and watch your Ps and Qs or you could go the other way. As Eamonn said, 'if you can't slag each other', then what do you do. And if you stop making jokes about people with disabilities, then you have to stop making jokes about people who are able-bodied. They don't want to be treated any differently. Eamonn was a lovely fellow and a successful businessman. Here was someone whose disability was never going to slow him down or hold him back."

Not that they could have anticipated what lay ahead. Prior to the *Lord Nelson*, Brennan's seafaring was of the limited and commercial variety. "My only experience on a ship was the Dun Laoghaire to Holyhead ferry doing a bit of Christmas shopping," he says. He never found his sea-legs during the rocking and rolling few days in the Mediterranean. "The minute I stood on the boat I felt unwell. It was like I was floating on air. I felt weak and light-headed and had double vision and was thinking, 'Jesus how am I going to get through this?'"

During his rugby playing days, Brennan was always the player who did the unexpected. He tells a tale from his Toulouse days. "It was after the semi-final against Leicester during my second year at the club," he says. "I was in another European Cup Final and I asked Fabien Pelous how I ended up in Toulouse with all its legendary players. He looked at me, took a sip of his pint and reeled off what each player brought to the team. How William Servat pin-pointed his man for the line-out throw, how Jauzion was brilliant in breaking the line, how Michalak was unerring with his kicks. He went through the whole team that way. And finally he said, 'then we come to you Trevor ... you just bring complete fecking havoc!'

In a way, during his five nights and six days on the *Lord Nelson*, Trevor Brennan also brought a certain type of havoc. First he snagged the lower bunk: leaving Eamonn to the upper limits. "Oh of course I did," he says without pause. "It was prison rules I told him. I was taking the bottom bunk whether he had one leg or two (he laughs). I said to Eamonn that's just the way it goes. In fairness to Eamonn though we got on like a house on fire. It was like meeting someone you knew for years. It wasn't someone that I had to watch my Ps and Qs around. I was worried about that beforehand. He was able to slag me just as well as I slagged him."

According to Eamonn Victory, the only time his ship mate ever popped his head above deck to work was when there was a camera in the vicinity. "He wasn't fecking lying!," Brennan says and laughs. "There was such a mix of people on the ship. There was young, there was old, there was soldiers, there was able-bodied people and disabled people but everybody mucked in and did everything. No matter what your disability was, whether you were blind or had one arm or one leg, you still made the effort to sail the ship. And that included everything from cooking to cleaning the ship."

For Trevor Brennan – a man with a few stories to tell himself – the story that *Two For the Road* told appealed to him. "I liked that it was highlighting the fact that people with a disability, whether they are missing an arm or a leg or are partially sighted or whatever, are no different from anybody else. They can still do things that able-bodied do and sometimes better. There's also the thing that some people feel uncomfortable around people with a disability in that they tend to stare at them. But I found in my experience on the *Lord Nelson* that all these people had a story to tell.

"Today I met a man who only fell blind in the last six years. I also talked with some soldiers who had been in Afghanistan and lost limbs. All these had all been able-bodied people who had to adapt to life and live with their disability. I found them and their stories incredible. Of course there were a couple of eejits on the trip as well who were bragging about how many people they killed."

(from Trevor's *Lord Nelson* diary)

Brennan's nominates his greatest rugby moment as his first ever cap for Ireland. "It will always be that moment," he says of his international debut in June 1998. "It wouldn't have been one of my most memorable matches because we got hammered by South Africa 37 to 13. But you work so hard through your career with people always saying that you could possibly play for Ireland one day. Then when you do, when you put on that jersey and run out for your country it is something special. But saying that there's also winning my first European Cup against Perpignan and winning again two years later are also highlights."

He probably dreamt of those days when he was rolling around in his hammock on the *Lord Nelson*. Days like the 2003 Heineken Cup Final. It was Toulouse versus Perpignan in Lansdowne Road and even if the crowd was a long way from capacity – a mere 2,000 Toulouse fans travelled to Dublin – the team decided that their lone Irish player had to lead them out. "I wasn't the captain that day, Fabien Pelous was," says Brennan. "But the night before the game they came to me and said: 'tomorrow you will lead out the team.' I said to them, don't be stupid but they were insistent. So the next day they let me run out first where I was on my own for what seemed like minutes. I ran about waving to everyone and then turned around to say, 'C'mon lads, let's get stuck into them!'. But there was no one there!'.

Before *Two For the Road*, the closest Trevor Brennan got to something outside his normal rugby playing sphere was the lifestyle show, *Hanging With Hector*. Now he was hanging over the side of a boat. But he admired the show's concept and the brave new world he was experiencing. "We take so many things for granted like walking or running up the stairs but life can be hard," he says. "Sometimes people look at people with a physical disability differently. I might have even done it myself, unconsciously, before I went on that trip but now I would have no hesitation in asking someone what happened to their leg or how they got their disability. In that confined space on the *Lord Nelson* I think I eventually discovered everybody's story and why they were on the boat."

He lists the highlight of the *Lord Nelson* voyage as pulling up on dry land. Joking apart there were other moments of light relief like the sing-songs in the ship's bar (Brennan is a master of such occasions from his own hostelry) but the trip was probably harder in a way than any rugby game he ever played. "To be honest with you I didn't enjoy the experience because I was so sick," he says. "Yet at the same time you dug deep because you knew that you were going home in a few days and these people have to live their disability for the rest of their lives."

Trevor Brennan lives in Toulouse with his wife Paula and their three children: Daniel (12), Joshua (9) and Bobby (4). He owns and runs the De Danu restaurant-bar near the city centre and since 2010 co-owns another establishment with former French and Toulouse hooker, William Servat. Since he left rugby his only involvement with the sport is a purely commercial one. In 2009 he set up Trevor Brennan Rugby Tours with two friends and since then has run a number of tours to Ireland (for the French internationals), to Cardiff (Leinster's 2011 Heineken Cup Final) and to New Zealand for the 2011 World Cup. "It's all about having the craic," he says of the tours. "That's my only involvement in rugby now."

At the beginning of March 2007 Trevor Brennan retired from rugby re-empting the decision of the ERC. It was an ignominious end to a mercurial and sometimes brilliant career. But he's still a sporting icon in his adopted home of Toulouse and he's not in any doubt that rugby gave him the best days of his life. "So many kids dream about playing for their province or playing for their country but I managed to get it all," he says. "I was captain of St Mary's RFC when they won the AIL League. I played for my country 13 times. I'd have loved to have played a bit more but that didn't happen. I played in three Heineken Cup Finals and two French finals. It's been ninety per cent good for the ten per cent that was bad."

"I don't think I'd go to sea on a tall ship again. Certainly if I was asked to do a documentary like that again, I wouldn't do it on a boat. I was never as sick in all my life."
(from Trevor's *Lord Nelson* diary)

While he is adamant that you'll never catch him on a tall ship again, Trevor Brennan concedes that the experience was an eye-opening one. "It made me appreciate what I have," he says. "The old saying that your health is your wealth is so true. I was able to do a lot of things that some of the physically disabled crew were unable to do, but their courage and fortitude amazed me. One man I spoke with, who was visually impaired told me that he had three daughters and seven grandchildren and he had never seen any of them. That's an amazing story. I have three kids myself and I couldn't imagine not knowing what they look like."

Eamonn's Story

"I was just 26 years old. I had a mortgage, I had a young child and I had been married just a couple of years. I asked the surgeon what would he do and he said that he'd take it off and get on with his life and that's what I did."

IN 1992 EAMONN VICTORY'S LIFE changed when his right leg was amputated just above the knee. And yet the change also gave him a motto of 'just get on with living' and he hasn't looked back. He now owns and runs the Centra supermarket in Dunleer County Louth with his wife, Sharon. He has skiied in Europe and in the US, he hasn't been out of work in the eighteen years since his operation and he's always looking to try something new. A week on the Lord Nelson sounded like it was just the ticket.

Originally from County Meath (Breffni Park), Eamonn Victory now lives in Grangebellew just outside Dunleer with Sharon and their three children: Sarah (20), Conor (15) and Andrew (7). He says that his wife, who runs the administrative side of the business, is his rock. The year after his amputation he opened the Dunleer shop with his father, who had been in the grocery business half a century. Then twelve years ago, when his father retired, he bought the business outright.

The reason for the amputation was a malignant tumour on his right knee that, despite being removed a number of times, kept growing back. Fearing that it might turn cancerous, and with the wounds taking longer and longer to heal, Eamonn had to make a big decision. "We had a new child and I was having an operation on my leg nearly every week for six or seven months. I was 26, I had a mortgage, I had a young child and just a couple of years married. I asked the surgeon what would he do and he said that he'd take it off and get on with his life and that's what I did."

After the surgeon's advice to have the leg amputated, Eamonn and his wife accepted its logic and necessity but it was still a traumatic moment. "Sharon and I came home that night, it was a Tuesday, and we cried our eyes out. But we never really spoke about it since. The thing is 'what do you do?' Sit on your arse and moan? A good few years later I came across a lovely poem from D H Lawrence (*Self Pity*). It goes: "I never saw a wild thing sorry for itself./ A small bird will drop / frozen dead from a bough / without ever having felt sorry for itself."

Six months after the operation Eamonn Victory was back at work having had a prosthetic leg fitted. "It was initially very sore because it cuts into your leg and the stump is painful," he says. "But you just have to get used to it. I suppose the other thing is that you get into bad habits and don't walk the way you should because you're dying to get to places as quick as possible. I remember my surgeon telling me, 'you don't give a damn how you get from A to B just as long as you get there as quick as possible'. I said 'not really!' I wasn't worried about posture or gait or being careful of my prosthetic leg."

But he reckons that he's lucky to be that kind of guy: a man who gets on with business. If he has low moments – and he jokes these happen every few minutes – he has his own way of coping. "If I think that if I'm getting down I'll time myself. So I'll feel bad for 15 minutes or whatever and then say, 'come on, get out of it.' But I would give myself that space and not plunge forward without recognising or dealing with those feelings. I gave that exact advice to another man who lost his leg: I told him to give himself some time, punch the air metaphorically or whatever, and then get on with it."

Eamonn Victory first met Edel Reck back in the mid 1990s during a trip to Crested Butte, Colorado. Since that adaptive skiing adventure, he has also skied in France and Italy. "The skiing was hugely challenging on one leg," he says. "You have crutches with little skis on the end of them and on your good leg you have a ski. There's a little string on the crutches that allows you to manipulate them so that you can turn and stop and stand. You take your prosthetic leg off. It's very painful. You need to be as fit as a fiddle for that. On one occasion I brought my young lad, Conor, with me and that was brilliant."

Over the past decade Edel kept him informed of plans to shoot a TV series about people with physical disabilities. When the green light was finally given in 2010, he was told that his adventure would be on board the *Lord Nelson*. "I don't get to mix with disabled people that often if at all and there were so many disabled people on the *Lord Nelson*. For me that was an eye-opener, to see disabled people in action – crying and laughing and getting sick and having the craic. I think that the more the public see disabled people in all aspects of their lives, the better."

Like Trevor Brennan the only boat he spent much time on was the ferry between Dublin and Holyhead. When Yellow Asylum Films contacted him, they told him his challenge and furnished him with some reading material which he didn't look at until the days before the trip. "You really don't get a sense of what it is about until you arrive at the dock in Las Palmas and see the *Lord Nelson* there in front of you," he says. "It's a beautiful ship outside and inside. It had an elegance and it said 'adventure' but it never occurred to me that we would have to work. I thought I'd be sipping beers on the deck with Mister Brennan!"

"The first thing I noticed on the boat was that they were unloading the food from a truck on the harbour. Everybody was getting involved. I was thinking then if this trip was going to be handy this would have been done already. So it was an ominous beginning in that respect."

(from Eamonn's *Lord Nelson* diary)

Once on board, lifejackets were handed out and assignments were detailed. "When we were given our watch duties, that was a bit of a reality check." His other reality check was his 'buddy'. "Trevor's the kind of lad that I like. He is all up-front and there's no holding back but at the same time there's no badness in him. He's a genuine chap. We got on well and we had a good old craic. He's an ugly git though and a bit tardy. If there was a camera there, no bother, Trevor would be there. But no camera, no Trevor!"

"We got all the stuff on board and then had a meeting with the captain. He was a funny kind of guy. Although he was very knowledgeable he was very informal about the trip and that was slightly disconcerting. We then got our duties and that was somewhat unexpected as well. Then we got sick. Then we went to bed. At midnight we got up for the night watch."

(from Eamonn's *Lord Nelson* diary)

The *Lord Nelson* 'threw up' different challenges. Sailing out of Las Palmas, the ship immediately hit rough weather. "I'd say that we were only out an hour and I just puked my guts up," he says. "I had to get to bed straight away. Of course I should have been on the bottom bunk where all the disabled people were but Brennan wouldn't let me in it. So I was on the top bunk. But when I got in there it was almost womb-like in its warmth. I felt good and comfortable in that hammock."

Just before midnight, his watch leader shook him awake. Below him Brennan wasn't budging. "I was thinking then, I don't really need to do this," says Victory. "But I knew that if I didn't get up I'd ruin the whole week because I wouldn't get involved. So I dragged myself up on deck while Brennan stayed where he was. I sat down in the darkness and it was rough. Even so I enjoyed the stillness of that night and being on watch. I pushed myself to get over the sickness and was delighted that I made the watch."

> *"The first night we sailed past Tenerife in the darkness and all you could see were the lights of the island. It seemed to float on the sea, almost like a floating city. It was fabulous."*
>
> (from Eamonn's *Lord Nelson* diary)

The next morning there was no respite. It was more of the same with the time spent scrubbing the decks and cleaning the heads (toilets). But by this stage Eamonn was beginning to find his sea legs. Just as well because later that day he had to 'go aloft' – climb up the rigging to the main mast. "I couldn't go up to the top because you have to lean back to climb up the last bit and I just couldn't do it," he says. "I was too weak and I got nervous."

The following day he tried again. This time he was supported with a safety harness but the downside was that his buddy had already climbed up ahead – the camera was rolling! – and was now shouting rugby-style words of encouragement to his climbing colleague. "I felt more comfortable that second day but Trevor was wrecking my head as I climbed up," he says. "He was yelling all this motivation jargon at me which was making me laugh more than anything else. But he's the salt of the earth. If you fell into the water he'd be the first one in after you."

In between the high seas and the hard work, there were moments of quiet when friendships were forged and stories were

swapped. For Eamonn Victory it was the people on the ship – from the partially sighted couple, to the soldiers who lost their limbs in war zones – who were the highpoint of the voyage. "I personally don't meet a lot of disabled people so I don't get that opportunity to sit down and talk with them for an hour to hear about their lives and the tragedies they have endured. Some of the lads who had injuries, the amputees, were very young and that struck me particularly."

All the time he was being slagged by his buddy: he was the 'cripple' but it was water off a duck's back. "It didn't bother me at all because I make fun of myself as well," he says. "I was a bollocks before I lost my leg; now I'm a one-legged bollocks. I can take it from Trevor and it's good crack but maybe others listening to those exchanges might have had a problem with it. But I'm a great believer in taking the piss out of disabled people because for me humour works because it hits the mark. If you can't laugh you might as well cry."

Eamonn Victory's attitude has always been a can-do one. He says that he's lucky that he's never been out of work since his leg was amputated – "having too much time on your hands can be bad" – but you sometimes make your own luck. "If I hadn't got up off my ass I'd still be getting sympathy. But the minute you get up off your ass the sympathy is gone. That's the way it should be. You get sympathy because you're sitting there doing nothing but if you're busting yourself working 70 or 80 hours a week no one is going to treat you any differently."

His week on the *Lord Nelson* was something he'd never have chosen himself but he believes that he'll be back some day, maybe with one of his children. "Being on the *Lord Nelson* made me realise in one way how small the world is," he says. "Or at least it made the world seem smaller. I thought that I would never have any association with the war in Afghanistan and then I met five soldiers who had been severely injured because of that conflict. On the *Lord Nelson* I got to see into other people's lives that I would never dreamed of looking inside. That was the thing I most enjoyed on the *Lord Nelson*."

CHAPTER SIX

Maeve Higgins and Sinéad Kane

Maeve Higgins

Maeve Higgins is from Cobh, County Cork. She has one brother, six sisters and two parents and has been making people laugh (for fun and sometimes money) for some time. As a writer and performer of stand-up comedy, Maeve has performed at a number of prestigious festivals across the planet including the Edinburgh Fringe Festival, the Melbourne International Festival and the Cat Laughs Festival, Kilkenny. She is also a familiar face and voice on TV and radio. However she is, is some ways, an accidental comedian. She just hopes she's not an accidental horsewoman.

Sinéad Kane

Sinéad Kane grew up in the town of Youghal, County Cork. She was born with only 5% vision in each eye and as a teenager considered a career in hotel management or radio presentation. But after being bullied in school she developed a strong inner determination and self-belief. She was the first blind person in Ireland to qualify as a solicitor. That drive and determination was to prove invaluable in a ranch in Mexico.

The Location

Rancho Las Cascadas is an equestrian ranch some 90 minutes from Mexico City and bordered by three waterfalls (Las Cascadas). It is situated on a central mountain plateau, 7,500 feet above sea level and thus the temperatures are somewhat cooler. The ranch comprises a mini conurbation of low-lying buildings including hacienda style guesthouses, a lounge area, a library, a billiard room, a bar and an open kitchen, all surrounded by manicured gardens.

Rancho Las Cascadas is run by Swiss-born Uschi Wiprächtiger and the multi-lingual staff are skilled in various disciplines from horsemanship to cooking and guitar-playing. The ranch accommodates every level of rider, from beginner to expert to those with a physical disability. The riding is exceptional in a special plateau dotted with wildflowers and cacti and punctuated with babbling streams and those landmark waterfalls. "The ranch was an extraordinary place," says Alan Gilsenan. "Not only was it really beautiful but it was run so well by Uschi, this incredibly wise, gentle and strong woman. You had a sense that this was a place that was also very much of Mexico. All the staff had a real pride in their work and in the ranch. Uschi was a very inspirational woman in lots of ways."

The Challenge

Sinéad Kane always wanted to horse ride. Maeve Higgins never thought much about it. Both of them were beginners. At the ranch they were able to use special mounting blocks that helped them get into the saddle. A number of wranglers, headed by Uschi, were on hand to help. To mimic the visual experience of Sinéad, Maeve wore a blindfold on her second time out horse riding. The experience was memorable, if not always in a totally positive way, for both riders.

The Shoot

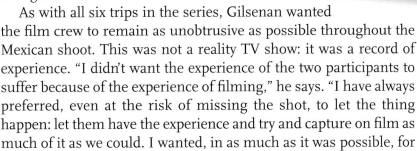

Alan Gilsenan had been horseriding before but had never been to Mexico before November 2010. In fact, the filmmaker admits, he really had no interest in visiting the North American country. Rancho Las Cascadas changed all that.

As with all six trips in the series, Gilsenan wanted the film crew to remain as unobtrusive as possible throughout the Mexican shoot. This was not a reality TV show: it was a record of experience. "I didn't want the experience of the two participants to suffer because of the experience of filming," he says. "I have always preferred, even at the risk of missing the shot, to let the thing happen: let them have the experience and try and capture on film as much of it as we could. I wanted, in as much as it was possible, for the two people to have an authentic experience and we would capture as much of that as we could. Otherwise the thing just becomes an exercise."

So Maeve and Sinéad were by and large left to their own devices. As the cameras rolled – shooting from the back of a pick-up truck for the action sequences, quietly filming for the girls' ranch area chats – they got to know each other and occasionally there was an edge to their interaction. "This was probably the only time in the series there was a bit of friction between the two travellers," says Gilsenan. "On the face of it Sinéad and Maeve seem to have a lot in common: they are of a similar age and they are both from Cork. And they did. But there were moments of tension, somewhat similar to that between two sisters in that there was never a lack of affection. It probably comes from the fact that both Maeve and Sinéad, in their own individual ways, would say it as it is. But it was good that they could talk about the issues they had with each other without losing fondness for each other."

If Gillsenan hoped to stay out of the frame, there was one moment when he had to momentarily step into the picture. It happened when Maeve's horse – she was wearing a blindfold for the first time – accidentally moved towards Sinéad's causing her to get

quite upset. "We weren't filming but we heard on the radio mikes that something was happening," says Gilsenan. "Sinéad got the impression that the horse was backing into her and she panicked and then fainted. She was very freaked by that incident. Maeve was riding a horse blindfolded for the first time in her life and may have been thinking why is Sinéad making such a scene. It was like a real moment where Maeve was so fed up, but then she thought, maybe that's unfair, because she has that ability to take off the blindfold. So that asked questions of any kind of device like this. How profound can a show like this really be because there's always that 'get out' clause, the sense that you can never really understand it truly."

But as Gilsenan discovered during his time in Rancho Las Cascadas, this *Two For the Road* episode became the story of a relationship as much as anything else. Ultimately the device of the blindfold triggered questions about what it means to be physically disabled or partially sighted. "We could have blindfolded Maeve for the whole trip in Mexico but I think that somehow that would have been a little patronising or diminished the experience," says Gilsenan. "So it became more about the relationship and they explored as little or as much of the disability as they were comfortable with. Now it might have been a more exciting TV programme if I had introduced a bit of *X Factor* stuff but that really did not seem right. It just seemed too gimmicky."

Maeve's Story

"I don't do many things that involve the word celebrity because those things are almost always mortifying and cringe inducing, but I was broke last winter. Just joking! I was interested in the idea of Two For the Road as I had never met a visually impaired person, never been to Mexico and never said yes to something like it before."

(from Maeve's Mexico diary)

"I NEVER REALLY KNEW what I wanted to do in life," says Maeve Higgins. "That used to really annoy me – and my parents! Eventually I studied photography at Coláiste Dhulaigh in Coolock in Dublin and I was really bad at it. But luckily in my final year I entered a radio competition on Today FM where they were looking for new stand-up comedians. I didn't win – it was my first time doing it and I was pretty terrible – but I fell in love with stand-up then. That was the only time I figured out what to do with myself."

Maeve Higgins grew up in the coastal town of Cobh – a short train ride from Cork city.

Apart from a brief brush with some Eddie Murphy stand-up DVDs, comedy was an alien and almost unreachable notion. "If you're a young girl from Cobh, County Cork watching that you're not going to think, 'oh, I can do that!'," she says. "At the time I thought Eddie Murphy was really good but now I think he's awful. But watching that DVD back then it put me off the idea of stand-up because I just thought it was for shouty guys. So yes I'm surprised that I ended up becoming a comedian."

But if the idea of doing comedy for a living was not considered in those early years, nothing else was really on the agenda either. "I was one of those kids who just did not know what to do with themselves," she says. "I didn't want to become a terrible scientist or a really rubbish nun or something so I just decided to do the vaguest thing I could think of doing which was photography because it sounded really easy and you don't have to stretch yourself. I was just lazy. I didn't really want to be a photographer or anything. I just didn't want to work. I was only 19."

She chose photography because she reckoned, 'how hard can that be?'. Then towards the end of that venture in 2004 she heard about a competition for fresh new comics on Today FM. So she gave it a lash, and loved it. "I didn't win but one of the producers rang me a few months later and asked me whether I'd be interested in doing a slot on their radio show," she says. "That was an amazing break because I'd only started doing comedy." That same year marked the beginning of her brilliant career as comedian with a couple of memorable performances. Or, as she writes in her website, "once on a bus outside a hotel in Cork and once in a room over a pub in Dublin."

She worked on all three series of the award-winning RTÉ hidden camera show, *Naked Camera*, from 2005 to 2007. "In the beginning I was still working in a clothes shop but then I went full-time into comedy in 2006 and I have been a full-time stand-up comedian since," she says. Apart from *Naked Camera* she had a regular slot on *The Ray D'Arcy Radio Show* on Today FM – 'What would Maeve Do?' offered unasked for advice to those facing social dilemmas and crises of etiquette.

In Autumn 2009, Maeve made one series of the TV show *Fancy Vittles* with her sister, Lilly, with whom she had worked at the Edinburgh Fringe Festival on the show *Ha Ha Yum*. *Fancy Vittles* was a clever and frequently hilarious ratatouille of food, relationships and archive footage in which the sisters teased out such overwhelming questions as what to do when your boyfriend breaks up with you, and the importance of chopped radish in a green salad.

Now we have Maeve Higgins horseriding in Mexico? It sounds like it could be the punchline for one of the comic's sketches. Adventure sports, or even non adventure sports, are not quite her thing. "To be honest I'm really not brave," she admits. "There was one time I got the train to Nenagh. I didn't even know where Nenagh was but I don't think that counts as an adventure or makes me an adventurous spirit. Sinéad in contrast has achieved so much, both academically and physically. She also looks after her mum who is one hundred per cent blind. She brings her out and about and is her guide. So compared to Sinéad I'm pretty rubbish. I'm just a comedian who doesn't do anything for anybody else."

But the comedian did agree to *Two For the Road* despite some initial scepticism – and a slight suspicion that she may have been at the end of a long list. Her main concern was that it would be seen as a vehicle just to boost her 'celebrity'. That and the scary fact that she would be blindfolded riding a horse. No mean challenge for someone whose usual activity is 'reading indoors' and 'sitting down after my gigs'.

Maeve met Sinéad the first morning after she arrived at Rancho Las Cascadas. If Maeve worried about being seen as a celebrity, they were unfounded as far as her travelling companion was concerned. Sinéad hadn't a clue who she was – apart from what she had gleaned from the web.

"It was funny at the start because Sinéad, I think, had never heard of me and I thought that was just brilliant. She was very polite about it but did quiz me early about the extent to which I knew Des Bishop. I said he was a friend, she asked if he'd ever been to my house, I said he had once and that helped to convince her I was worthy of the title 'celebrity'."

(from Maeve's Mexico diary)

Before meeting Sinéad, Maeve had never known a partially sighted person. She was thus, like most people, unaware of the world that her companion inhabited. Her experience was all second-hand, something she only glimpsed at the periphery of day-to-day life whether that was a blind person getting on a bus, or someone using a guide dog to negotiate a street crossing. With Sinéad, she saw up close how every little bit of life is changed when you can only see so much of the world. "It was a real wake-up call for me," she says. "Even doing things like putting on make-up which I'd take for granted. Myself and Sinéad talked about that quite a bit early on and I thought, my God, that's a really tricky thing to do when you can't see. In a way that crystallised how difficult many aspects of Sinéad's life must be."

"That morning, Sinéad took me aside for a chat off camera and explained how she had been bullied in school because of her visual impairment, by teachers and students alike. She also said she qualified as a solicitor despite various people expressing doubts about her ability and how proud she was of that. It was a pretty heavy conversation for the first time we ever met, but it showed me she means business! Her life experience was very different to mine. I sort of drifted into my work and have never needed to fight against anything, so I definitely felt a lot of respect for her that morning."

(from Maeve's Mexico diary)

Maeve's horse was named Calypso: a gentle soul like all horses on the ranch. But unlike their compatriots in Europe these horses didn't 'do' trotting. "They go from walking to cantering to running," she says. "So it was really hard to stay in the saddle. We were flying all over the place. "

"My horse, Calypso, was unreal. He was so beautiful, copper coloured and in the prime of his life. I am not used to horses at all but I swear I loved him the second I met him. He was so strong and calm and I

*trusted him immediately. The days I wore a blindfold I knew that
Calypso wouldn't let me come to any harm, and he didn't."*

(From Maeve's Mexico diary)

On the first day Maeve went riding without any physical restrictions: simply getting to know Calypso and the terrain. Then in the afternoon of the following day the blindfold was put on and suddenly she was thrown into a disorientating and sometimes scary place. "The hardest part was not knowing where everybody else was," she says. "I trusted the horse not to fall into a ravine or jump into a load of cactus or whatever. So I trusted my horse to keep me safe but I couldn't tell where everybody else was. That was one aspect of being blindfolded that I didn't think would bother me. I just thought I'd hear their voices. But I was really thrown by how I couldn't see anybody else. It was a bit scary. I was scared of not being able to communicate."

On that afternoon, Maeve and Sinéad set out with Uschi and the crew. Both were effectively riding unsighted. Maeve, wearing the blindfold, was initially unable to tell whether her mount was moving backward or forward as her senses were thrown into disarray. Then both horses made contact ...

"Everything was going great until Calypso and I almost brushed off Sinéad and her horse and caused her to completely lose the plot. I didn't realise until after that how much Sinéad's visual impairment affects her experience. I don't think Sinéad ever fully believed she was safe on her horse, which is a shame, because she was. She carried on though, fair play, and we had a brilliant time."

(from Maeve's Mexico diary)

After her time in Rancho Las Cascadas, Maeve discovered that she was calmer than she believed herself to be. But on the downside she reckons, that she's pretty blinkered in what she understands about other peoples experiences of the world. Spending time with Sinéad reinforced this belief. "I would have thought that I'm quite empathetic but that week I spent with Sinéad surprised, indeed shocked me," she says. "I realised how little I had considered other people's experience. So I reckon I'm quite immature because I get surprised when people have a different opinion to me! I don't get challenged as much in my daily life as I did on that adventure with Sinéad."

"I learned a lot about visual impairment and the impact it has on lives. Another good thing that has come out of the show for me is that I've taken up horse riding here in Ireland, though I haven't come across an equal to Calypso just yet."

(from Maeve's Mexico diary)

Since she returned from Mexico, Maeve Higgins has been busy with gigs and writing new material and pitching a TV pilot. But she has also found time to go horse-riding. "I really did fall for the horses in a big way," she says. "I just can't believe how sweet and brave they are. We didn't do it alone. It was the horses and the people at the ranch who really helped us. I just love horses now. I didn't realise before how intuitive they are and I think that they looked out for Sinéad and for me. They didn't let either of us fall or get injured. Nothing bad happened and that was down to the horses and not my great riding skills."

Sinéad's Story

"My family's house was situated on a very steep hill. Little did I know when I was born that this steep hill would represent the journey of struggle that I would encounter though my life."

(from Sinéad's Mexico diary)

FROM AN EARLY AGE Sinéad was her mother's eyes: helping her to negotiate the nooks and crannies of their home as well as navigate the wider world. In a way it was a sort of payback as Sinéad was aware of the sacrifice her mother made before she was even born. "When she was pregnant with me my mother was referred to a hospital in London where she was told that she would lose her eyesight totally within the year," she says. "She was told that if she were to have the child, her eyesight would deteriorate much more quickly than if she didn't have the child. She decided to go ahead and had me and then she lost her sight."

In a way by helping her mother, Sinéad's mobility and spatial awareness was dramatically improved beyond the norm. According to medical staff she should be using a white cane or a guide dog but all her life she has managed perfectly well without either. This independence is something she values but also, one suspects, something she has earned. "I think that if you grow up in a situation where people fuss over you and you allow that to happen then you begin to think 'I can't do this' and you fall into the trap of allowing others do it for you."

Back in those teenage years she had dreams of going into hotel management or becoming a radio presenter. The former because she like meeting people, the latter because it would give her a voice and a large audience. "I grew up in an environment where I felt that I wasn't being listened to in terms of my educational rights," she says. "I got bullied at school because of my disability. That had a very big impact on me. In fifth year I was out of school for six months because of stress and sickness. I started to learn then about law and my rights so I turned it all around and decided that people would not walk over me any more. I decided that people were not going to tell me what I could or could not achieve. I became a more positive person then."

After school Sinéad studied law at UCC from 2001 to 2004 when she graduated with a BCL. The following year she completed a Masters in Law (LLM) and remained at the university for a further year to teach law to people with disabilities. Then, from 2006 to 2009, she did her solicitor training with the Law Society of Ireland. Sinéad Kane was the first qualified partially sighted solicitor in Ireland. She hopes to open up her own practice or else gain a management position in the public or private sector.

"In an interview with Alan Gilsenan he asked me what I thought was the biggest misconception about people with disabilities. I replied that people with disabilities are perceived as stupid and that we spend all the time inside our houses feeling sorry for ourselves. I told Alan that when I was young I was bullied and made ashamed of my disability. Whereas now as an adult I accept myself and embrace my disability as a positive aspect of my life."

(from Sinéad's Mexico diary)

Sinéad sees herself as more academic than sporty: someone whose greatest sporting achievement prior to horse riding in Mexico was a mini marathon ("a rare event") and a climb on Mt Krizevac in the Bosnia-Herzegovina pilgrimage shrine of Medjugorje. "That was tough," she says. "I was saying to my friends on the way up that I thought that I wasn't going to make it. I was thinking in my head that this mountain symbolises my life in that there are so many rocks along the way. You just want to give up but if you give up you don't get to the top of the mountain."

When she was first approached about getting involved in *Two For the Road*, Sinéad was immediately up for it even though she did not know what the challenge would be. But her overriding worry from the outset was that she might not be able to do it, a fear fuelled by her 'perfectionist' nature and her self-critical mindset. Then when she heard that her companion would be a stand-up comedian she was even more nervous: worried that her disability would be ridiculed or made fun of. However she was equally prepared to say straight up what was on her mind because that's just the way she is and she could not be untrue to herself. So their first meeting was very much a sounding out.

"Maeve was sitting across the round table from me so it was hard to see her but I could tell a lot by the tone of her voice. Instantly I knew that she was a 'quirky' type. I could tell by the tone of her voice her different facial expressions, for example when she was smiling and when she wasn't. Sometimes I fear meeting new people because I worry that they will judge me due to my disability."

(from Sinéad's Mexico diary)

What was Maeve like? To Sinéad she was from the other side of the planet: a tomboyish and quirky individual.

"Maeve and I are quite different people, nearly like chalk and cheese. But that is what made my conversations with Maeve interesting. We both come from different backgrounds. We also have different values and beliefs and different interests and hobbies. But I think this is how people learn from one another. If you put two people who are very different together, it makes things more interesting."

(from Sinéad's Mexico diary)

Sinéad's mount, Palomo, was one of the quietest and gentlest horses on the ranch. "A poodle", as Sinéad later described him: a horse that wanted to take care of her. But that first time she stepped up to the mounting block to get onto the saddle, Sinéad was quaking inside, a situation made worse because she didn't want people to see that she was nervous. After all she was the strong, confident person who

beat the bullies and carved out her own successful career as a solicitor. So surely a little horse-riding was not all that big a deal?

"I thought to myself this horse is big and powerful. I am not going to
kick it because if I do it might make it mad. But I trusted Uschi and so
I put the reins over Palomo's head and kicked him on the side and he
then started to move away from the mounting block. Uschi told me
not to be afraid, to sit tall, sound confident and act like you deserve to
have your horse listen to you. Otherwise you will sit on an unmoving
horse for some time."

(from Sinéad's Mexico diary)

Sinéad's first day out was a rollercoaster of emotions. Not only was
she riding a horse for the first time but she was also riding a horse
through water: it was like her greatest fear magnified a million
times. Unnerved by the sound of the stream and anxious about how
deep it might be, she very nearly turned back. Sinéad's nightmare
that she might fall from the horse and thus incur a second disability
was very real in those moments. But under the gentle yet persuasive
guidance of Uschi she crossed the stream.

"There were so many emotions going through me in that
moment," she says. "Sadness, happiness, anger, sense of achievement, sense of 'I-can't-believe-this-is-happening' and all of that. I
suppose my biggest fear was not being able to see how deep the water
was. I thought that the horse was going to fall in the water because he
couldn't see where he was going. And if he fell, then I'd fall too. That
was the big fear. I was trying to explain that to the people around me
but they didn't seem to be listening. Then it felt like I was back at
school again: trying to explain
things to people who weren't
listening to me. When I got to
the other side, I felt that I had
done something great and I
needed time to take that in. It
was a huge deal to me."

The next day Maeve wore
a blindfold and her horse,
Calypso, seemed to brush

into Palomo, Sinéad got so upset that she had to be helped from her horse. Once she was standing on the ground she promptly fainted.

"It all happened really quickly but I started to getting this immense fear over me because I thought Maeve's horse was going to knock me off my horse and that I was going to get trampled on by the other horses."

(from Sinéad's Mexico diary)

As she can only see six foot in front of her, Sinéad's sense of scale was boxed into these limits. When she could feel Maeve's horse reversing into hers, she started to panic. "All I could think about was 'where are all these horses going to go?' That's why I started to panic. I then thought that I was going to fall and then I'd have the legs of the three horses trampling on me. Now it might seem silly to think that because we're out in a big wide area but when you can only see so far, you think that you're in small area." She got off, felt faint and collapsed. Afterwards she was angry with herself and embarrassed:

ashamed at getting upset and critical of herself. "I thought why didn't I get up on that horse quicker? When life knocks you down you can't stay knocked down; you have to get back up straightaway."

But she did. On her fourth and final evening in Mexico Sinéad rode Palomo back to the ranch through the darkness. The film cameras had stopped rolling and the film crew had all bundled into a truck. For Sinéad it had been a long and challenging few days. Now that final horse ride was an emotional one of freedom and release.

"That canter back to the ranch was the highlight for me. The wind in my face as Palomo was speeding along was an out-of-this-world feeling. I felt completely free, completely independent of all human help."

(from Sinéad's Mexico diary)

Sinéad Kane is now 29. She would like some day to have her own family but knows there is a risk that her children too might be visually impaired. There are also issues, born of personal experience. "I think to myself, do I want to put a child through the things that I experienced such as bullying and pain and sorrow?" she asks. "But then you balance it against all the good things I have achieved and the happiness I have brought into the world and my child can bring that as well."

A devout Roman Catholic Sinéad has visited a number of major pilgrimage sites including Lourdes, Medjugorje and San Giovanni Rotondo, the spiritual home of Padre Pio. "I do feel that God is working through me to show that good things can happen even though I have a disability," she says.

"Having faith is very important to me. Having faith gives a person hope. Hope that there will be life after death. Hope that even a 'disabled' person can overcome challenges. Hope that my disability wasn't given to me because I had offended God but more to educate people about the potential of people. I think that some people are given disabilities not because God is being evil but to show how much the human person is capable of."

(from Sinéad's Mexico diary)

Since she returned from Mexico she has taken a couple of riding lessons in Ireland, even if occasionally old prejudices resurface and she is 'advised' that maybe she should try a less demanding sport. She hopes that *Two For the Road* too will influence people with disabilities, challenge them to visit places like Rancho Las Cascadas and experience what she did. "Sometimes society tells people that they can't do certain things and people with disabilities then don't push themselves because they believe this," she says. "They really shouldn't."

"Overall my Mexico trip was a beautiful release for me from my disability. The memories have seeped into my veins and will remain there forever. Such memories will act like blood for me to keep me going when times are tough, when I am having a 'bad eye' day. The trip gave me great peace and I felt as if I was in the arms of an angel with Uschi watching over and protecting me all the time."

(from Sinéad's Mexico diary)

CHAPTER SEVEN

Ken Doherty and Seán Connick

Ken Doherty

Dubliner Ken Doherty is still the only snooker player to have won both the amateur (1989) and professional (1997) world championship – and he did it all with a warped cue! In the 2000 Masters he narrowly failed to record a maximum 147 break and win a high performance sports car. With Two For the Road he was getting his opportunity to drive one – and overcome his phobia of crashing.

Seán Connick

Seán Connick, the former Minister for State at the Department of Agriculture, Fisheries and Food was the first wheelchair user TD in Dáil Éireann when he was elected to the Wexford constituency in May 2007. For two years in his teens this self-described 'petrolhead' was a co-driver in a rally car. On Two For the Road he would be in the driving seat.

The Location

Chris Birkbeck's International Rallying School is in North Yorkshire, close by the seaside resort of Saltburn-by-the-Sea. The dramatic location overlooks the North Sea and is surrounded by a golf driving course. But this is a serious rally circuit that would test any driver as it includes nerve-shredding hairpins, speedy straights, car-lifting crests and a mixture of surfaces, from loose gravel to hard tarmac.

This rally day was facilitated by Cyclone Mobility (one of the UK's leading designers and manufacturers of wheelchairs) whose MD is Dave Hawkins, a paraplegic and successful rally driver. Dave drives a Subaru Impreza but he wasn't likely to loan that to the likely lads of Ken and Seán.

The Challenge

A two litre Opel Kadett sports car driven
over a rough and tumble circuit at speeds
of up to 80 miles per hour is tough
enough. Then you factor in the adapta-
tions. The Kadett was all hand controls with the throttle on the
steering wheel rim and the push/pull brake located alongside. For
both drivers it would be the first time using these type of controls.

The drivers were kitted out in fire-retardant suits and miked up
to their co-driver and navigator, Howard Paterson. There were a few
practice runs in the morning before the real deal, the time trial, in
the afternoon. At one point the crew considered restricting Ken's
legs but for safety reasons this was abandoned. The challenge was
carried out under the careful instruction, watchful eyes and nervous
feet of rally ace, Paterson.

The Shoot

"We had about five cameras rigged in the car and then we were
outside with two other cameras," says Alan Gilsenan. "In actual fact
it was rather easy and good fun because they were both natural
competitors. We were filming at one point and Ken came off the
track but it was no big deal and the instructor, Howard, who was
good fun, was also hugely capable."

For the first time in the series the film crew were in the firing line. At one point – when Ken Doherty took out a stack of tyres on a particularly sharp bend – they scurried for the safety of the heights where they stayed for the rest of the one day shoot.

There was also the unexpected elements like shooting high octane car racing while surrounded by the more pastoral element of golfing. As a result, when recording interviews, the filming had to pause while the golfers with their bags of clubs click-clacked past. And the night before the rallying, the crew planned to film a sequence in a pool hall in Hartlepool where Ken had arranged a challenge match with another pro player. But as the venue had no ramps and lifts for Seán the shoot had to be scrapped.

There were no such problems on the rally circuit. "Howard was very perceptive on Ken and Seán in analysing their driving," says Gilsenan. "He said that while they have very different backgrounds, they were both used to performing under pressure. You could see that as a snooker player and as a politician you had to have that ability to hold your nerve. He said that they both did and as a result were really good drivers."

Ken's Story

"AH JESUS it *was* scary," says Ken Doherty recalling his brief time as a rally driver. "Your heart pounds in snooker but it doesn't pound as much as it does when you're in a racing car going at 80 miles an hour down a dirt track. That's just frightening. There's also the frightening sound of all the stones flying up against the undercarriage of the car as you brake into a corner. It sounds like bullets coming out of a gun, it's that noisy."

Ken Doherty was a bit of a tearaway as a young lad and has the scars to prove it. "I was always getting into scrapes. I broke my arm, I fell off a roof, I got hit with hurley during a game and I nearly lost my eye when I was about fourteen. But the worst was when I fell off a garden shed roof when I was seven. I fell backwards onto a rusty bin and broke my arm in three places. I missed the mortar blocks by a couple of inches. If I hit them with my head I was gone. I cut all my face on the rusty bin itself and that's how I got the scar."

Growing up in Dublin in the early 1980s was not the best of times. But for Ken Doherty there was *Pot Black* on the TV (which he

watched with his dad, Tony) and Jason's snooker hall in nearby Ranelagh village. Beyond that establishment's front door were pool tables, a juke box and space invader machines, but it was the solitary snooker table by the window that fascinated young Ken. He was only ten when he first visited – his older brother Seamus had to chaperone him – but those first steps into the dark were to take him to the top of the world.

Ken Doherty was eight when he got his first snooker table and a few years older when he bought the cue – a warped specimen for £2 from the rack at Jason's – that he still plays with today. But in the beginning his mother didn't approve of his passion for the game. "I'd come home from school, throw the school bag under the table and that would be it – down to Jason's," he says. "Me ma would be around every day trying to drag me out of the place with her wooden spoon."

Andy Collins, the manager at Jason's, played a key role in Doherty's career. When the schoolboy was unable to pay, Collins gave him free practice in exchange for some housekeeping chores. "Andy wouldn't switch the light on over the table but I'd get a free game of snooker if I emptied the ash trays and swept the floor," he says. "So I had a warped cue, I had no light and I had to work for the one game. I also needed a biscuit tin to stand on because I was too small to reach the table. When I started beating some of the older players the biscuit tin would go missing the odd time!"

When he was thirteen, and just starting to make his mark in the game, Ken's dad, Tony, died. "That was in June 1983 and my first tournament was in August. After my father died they gave me free practice because they knew that my mother couldn't afford to have me in the snooker club. They obviously saw a bit of potential, particularly Andy who was really good. I had to keep this little diary on who I played and what the score was and my highest break and all that. It started with an hour's free and then it became free as long as I wanted. They sponsored me into tournaments around Ireland, paid for the travel and at the end they were giving a few bob as well."

After Jason's he worked at Goff's, home to Irish snooker. There he got to see his sporting icons up close – and sometimes even got to meet them. "I worked there for two or three years. I was meeting all these guys and watching them play live and it sort of gave me a great experience of the big stage and what it was like. It gave me a taste for it and made me want to work harder and want it more."

In 1985, at the age of fifteen, he lost the Benson & Hedges amateur championships. Four years later he won the Irish Amateur Championships which qualified him for the World Amateur in Singapore. He won, becoming World Amateur and World Junior champion in the same year. The win fastracked him into the pro ranks in 1990 but it would be three years before his first ranking win on the circuit (The Welsh Open) in 1993. For the next 15 years he would remain in the world's Top 16.

After a terrible start to the 1997 season, he was very long odds for the World Championship. But he potted opponent after opponent before toppling the then almost invincible Stephen Hendry 18 -12 in the final. "That win brought me back to when I was a kid watching the world championship with my dad," he says. "Watching Alex Higgins win in 1982, watching Dennis Taylor win in 1985. All those great memories came back to me. To be actually lifting the cup in front of the whole Crucible crowd was just what dreams are made of."

There was an open-top bus parade through Dublin city centre, a victory parade with the trophy at Croke Park, Old Trafford and Celtic Park and of course a triumphant homecoming to Jason's. But in the midst of all the celebrations, he remembered the man who introduced him to the sport. "All my memories came back to my dad because we used to watch the snooker together," he says. "He never saw me play in a competition. He only saw me play on the table that I got when I was eight and the six by three table which I used to play in the house. I'm sure he was looking down on me that night and willing me on."

In 2007 Ken Doherty became a father for the first time when his wife, Sarah, gave birth to Christian. "It changes you completely," he says of fatherhood. "Everything revolves around him. I even take him down the snooker club with me. He loves the snooker and hitting the balls. I have to get him a biscuit tin! He's only three and a half but I got him a little cue about 18 inches long and he hits Lego pieces with it. My wife's not too happy. She wants him to follow in her footsteps and be a doctor."

Ken Doherty had known Edel Reck, an avid fan and follower of professional snooker, for years. He was the first person to commit to her *Two For the Road* proposal. "I thought it was great," he says. "You're putting yourself in the shadow of that person with the disability. So while you realise how difficult it is for them to do certain things, you also realise how strong they are and how well they are able to cope. These people don't throw in the towel, they get on with life and enjoy it. That's what I found with Seán. He loves life, lives it to the full and works hard. He's also a better rally driver than I am!"

Like Seán Connick, Ken Doherty loves cars but his technical knowledge is limited. "I don't know a thing about them," he says. "Once I open up the bonnet that's about as far as it goes with me. I can put in the oil and water and fill the tank with petrol but ask me to change a plug or an air filter and I'd be lost. But I love cars and I love driving them."

Ken Doherty, who had done some Karting in his youth, but had only one experience of real rally driving before Saltburn when he participated in a charity event at Punchestown track. In that instance he was co-driver and not at the wheel. There was the time he came close to winning a classic sports car for a maximum 147 break in the 2000 Benson & Hedges Masters final but he missed the final black. "The car was a Honda NSX and worth about 100,000 euro," he says. "My excuse is that I didn't like the colour!"

Now in Saltburn-by-the-sea on a cool morning in March he was getting his opportunity at last.

"This morning I felt nervous. I didn't know what to expect and I didn't know how I was going to do: how good or how bad a driver I would be. I wasn't sure how dangerous it would be either so I was nervous for that reason. But I was also excited, like a kid in a sweet shop, because I got to put on all the rally kit. I looked like something out of Formula One. But the fact that you're getting into a car and travelling at high speed was quite nerve racking."

(from Ken's rally diary)

The specially adapted Kadett presented a few problems for the novice rallyer. "I couldn't use my legs so everything was done with my hands which was a little bit strange and took a while to get used to," he says. "The brake was beside the steering wheel, the throttle was on the steering wheel and my feet kept banging on the floor looking for the clutch and brake! In fact my leg was going all the time. And the co-driver's leg was going too especially when I was spinning out of control and heading for the ditch."

In the morning practice sessions it took Ken a while to get used to the controls and the car. At one point, on a tight corner, he spins off the circuit and clobbers a stack of tyres. "Did you see the camera crew running out of the way?," he asks. "They were on the hill making sure they were well out of the way when I was ripping it down the straight and making that hand-brake turn. Of course in that moment you'd always be afraid that the car might flip over."

At one stage there were plans to restrict Ken's leg movement to mimic Seán's situation but for safety issues this was decided against. "My heart was just popping out of my shirt as you're racing against the clock and you're spinning around corners and learning how to use the handbrake and keep control of the car. At the end of snooker matches you get this adrenaline rush because of the build up of pressure and the expectation of winning or the horrible sensation of possibly losing. Being in that car, flying down that track and spinning

into corners, was a similar rush."

For the time trial, the instructor mapped out a new circuit: a different course to the one they had been practicing on all morning. "He thought we had got used to that one so he threw a spanner in the works and set out a whole new track," says Doherty. "He gave us a couple of practices before he started the clock. It was very, very close. I was delighted for Seán because he was feeling a lot more down than I was after losing his seat."

"I don't like losing but I couldn't have lost to a nicer fellow. However Seán did gloat over dinner that he beat me by a second. We drank to that and I said to Seán that if this rallying happens again I'd like to challenge him to a rematch."

(from Ken's rally diary)

"It was quite a humbling experience because sometimes you can take your own health for granted," he says. "I might moan about losing a snooker match or get a bit down after losing a game and then you realise how hard it can be for someone with a disability. But you also realise how strong they are and how much you can learn from someone with a disability. They know that life is there to be enjoyed. That for me is what I took from the whole experience. These people are very strong, very brave and great characters."

Ken Doherty continues to play snooker with his warped cue. He

also owns and runs a snooker club in Terenure in Dublin. "It's called, erm, the Ken Doherty Snooker Academy," he says. "We put a lot of thought into the name as you can see! I hope to get a lot of young lads in so that we can give them a bit of coaching and maybe they can realise their ambition of becoming world champion. It has pool tables, a darts area and even a juke box – a bit like Jason's all those years ago. But there are no biscuit tins there. Yet."

Sean's Story

EXACTLY ONE WEEK after losing his seat and his junior ministry in the 2011 General Election, Seán Connick was sitting in a rally car on the north east coast of England. If that week had been a long time, politics were very far from his mind as he sat behind the wheel of a souped-up and specially modified Opel Kadett. With his wife, Lourde, watching, the 46-year-old was drilled on how to use the hand controls by his instructor, and co-driver, Howard Paterson. It was going to be a long day.

"That morning I had fear. I could hear the rally car being revved up outside and my mind was whirring with so many questions. 'How fast will we be going? 'Will I crash?' 'Will I manage it?' All those thoughts were running through my head. They are I suppose irrational fears. But that's what makes a good rally driver. The bad rally drivers are, I believe, the lads with no fear."

(from Seán's Rally diary)

Seán Connick was always mad about cars: driving them, reading about them and watching them on *Top Gear* (his favourite TV show). His father John was well known throughout South Wexford as a car dealer having got started in the motor industry in the early 1970s. In 1974 he opened his own garage in New Ross and eight year-old Seán was a regular visitor. Every summer holiday was spent working in the garage and later he worked full time on the premises for seven years. That was after he completed his Leaving Certificate in 1981 and long after the accident that changed his life.

It happened on the morning of 17 August 1977 (the date will never fade), ten days before his thirteenth birthday. Connick was cycling, with some friends, to a game of pitch and putt just outside the town. When he dropped some golf balls he went back to collect them. It was at a treacherous cross-roads and, momentarily distracted, he cycled into the path of an oncoming car. His injuries were horrific.

"Everything on my left side was basically broken," he says. "I had a compound fracture of my tibia and fibula, my thigh bone was also broken. When I came off the car I broke my back from the T4 through to the T7, the vertebrae were crushed at chest level. My ribs were obviously broke and I punctured a lung."

He was rushed to Waterford Hospital and then airlifted to the National Rehabilitation Hospital in Dun Laoghaire. For a couple of weeks it was touch and go whether he would live. He remained in hospital until Christmas and then was back for every week day until the following Easter. His recovery was slow and painful. "For me it was a case of first wanting to be able to sit up," he says. "Then to get into the wheelchair. Then just wanting to get home. There were progressive steps and that's what I was focusing on. Just getting back into the land of the living so to speak."

During his recuperation, Connick was never told that he would be using a wheelchair for the rest of his life. "No one ever said to me, 'you'll never walk again'. It's a great line in the films but I never had that conversation with anyone. I joke with my friends even now that one of these days someone is going to say to me, 'look Seán, you're paralysed.' But that conversation never happened. It did happen with my parents and they were devastated. For me it was a gradual realisation that there was something very serious wrong, that I couldn't feel my legs."

When he returned home, his parents and the school authorities at CBS New Ross decided that he should return to his old class and classmates rather than a lower class. Connick believes that this decision played a crucial part in his recovery. "I was Seán Connick to all of my classmates before the accident and now I was Seán Connick back again but in a wheelchair," he says. "I believe that if I had gone back a class I would have had to rebuild relationships. And those friends were great."

By then Seán Connick was well-known in New Ross – the news coverage of the accident was extensive - and was coming to terms with being 'famous' and being 'different'. "I lost my anonymity after the accident," he says. "No matter where I went people knew who I was. They would also look at the wheelchair. Things have changed since then but back in the '70s and '80s I was very conscious of being in a wheelchair. I was very conscious of the fact that I had been paralysed. I suppose there is an element of that still in me. You don't want people making a fuss of you. You just want to get on with it."

His love of cars was still as strong as ever and working in his father's garage he got to indulge his passion. But a car now had a greater significance for him. "The car is such a hugely important piece of equipment for me," he says. "Probably the most important piece of equipment outside of the wheelchair in terms of getting you around. I worked there for seven years and unfortunately we sold it on then in the middle of the last big recession in the late 1980s."

During his time in the garage he also did some rally driving. Together with a mechanic friend they converted a Fiat 127 Sport for racing and entered it for local and regional rallies for two years. "I sat in the passenger seat and called the notes," he says. More recently he and his wife Lourde have driven throughout Europe and South Africa and in 2009 they drove Route 66 and in the summer of 2010 completed an eastern circuit of Canada, starting and finishing in Toronto.

Lourde, who was also in Saltburn-by-the-sea, has been with Seán for thirty years. He was sixteen when they started dating, having met her at a *Tops of the Town* contest (he plays guitar) in 1981. Six years later they married. "She has stood by me the whole way," he says. "In a way Lourde is the driver when my engine goes down. We've had loads of ups and downs and challenges that we got over together. She is an amazing person and has always been by my side. She has been my best friend and my soul mate and my wife for the past twenty-four years now."

Rarely in his life has he felt aware of the physical and emotional limitations of his disability. "The first time in my life that I really felt disabled was when my dad died. My father died when I was 27 and he was only 54. At the time I was aware of my disability but it became much more real when my dad died. I don't why but that struck me at the time."

Another major time his disability impacted was when he and Lourde tried to have a family. "We pursued that vigorously back in the early 1990s for a period of about ten to twelve years," he says. "We checked out pioneering fertility treatments for people with spinal injury and I was one of those pioneers, travelling to Dublin on a frequent basis. But we weren't successful. It was something we always wanted but unfortunately it didn't happen."

Before his accident, Seán dreamed of following his father into the motor industry: hoping to own his own garage and sell cars. Later he briefly toyed with the notion of becoming an accountant before he joined his father in the garage. Eventually he set up his own businesses becoming a bona fide entrepreneur. So the subsequent drift into politics was 'unexpected'. He and his family, while long time Fianna Fáil supporters, had no background in political matters.

"In 1999 I was approached in New Ross by some of the local county councillors and asked whether I'd consider running. I was 34 years of age. They came back a few times to convince me. I just got stuck in and it snowballed. In 1999 I was in the town council. In 2004 I was in the town and county council. In 2005 I was president of the association of municipal authorities of Ireland. Then at the end of 2005 I got the nomination to run for the Dáil.'

In May 2007 Seán Connick became the first ever wheelchair user TD in Dáil Éireann, a historic win that required a number of physical alterations to the chambers and entrances. Lifts and ramps were installed, and both the Merrion Street and Kildare Street entrances were made wheelchair accessible. "I never traded on my disability as I didn't want to be pigeon-holed when I went into politics," he says. "But at the back of my head all the time I was in the Dáil I was thinking here is somebody with a disability who has achieved a very high office. I was always conscious that in a way I gave an element of confidence to people with disabilities by achieving what I had done."

But on Saturday, February 26, 2011, the junior minister was not re-elected (and subsequently failed in his attempt to get elected to the Seanad). It was then that a TV series he had agreed to do filled the void. "I lost my seat on the Saturday and the following Saturday I was filming in the North of England," he says. "At the time it was a welcome distraction because it is a very traumatic thing to lose a seat. It felt very personal and cut to the bone. People say that it's not personal but when it's your face on the ballot paper and you don't come through, you do feel it personally."

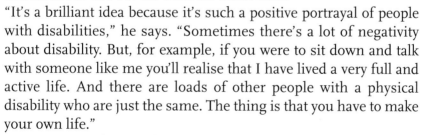

Through Edel Reck, Seán Connick had known about *Two For the Road* for some time. "It's a brilliant idea because it's such a positive portrayal of people with disabilities," he says. "Sometimes there's a lot of negativity about disability. But, for example, if you were to sit down and talk with someone like me you'll realise that I have lived a very full and active life. And there are loads of other people with a physical disability who are just the same. The thing is that you have to make your own life."

On *Two For the Road* he was offered a few options but passed on both skiing ("enough hardship in my life") and dog sledding ("I have a phobia of dogs") before settling for the obvious one: rallying. The added bonus was his 'opponent'. "I knew Ken from his World Championship win but to get to know him personally was great," he says. "He's a very funny fellow and very relaxed company."

On Saturday morning he saw the car. It was an Opel Kadett

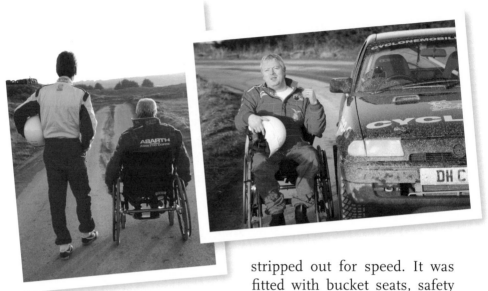

stripped out for speed. It was fitted with bucket seats, safety harnesses and fire retardant features. Both driver and co-driver wore microphones and fire protection suits. This was a real rally car and the first time that Seán was at the wheel. "The hand controls were different from what I would normally use," he says. "I would use a push-pull system whereas they were using a steering ring which is very effective because it allows you to keep your hands on the wheel."

The morning was a series of practice sessions around a variety of circuits. Hand-brake turns, braking and coping with the different surfaces – and the commands from the co-driver and instructor, Howard Paterson, a professional rally driver, occasional stunt man and full-time entertainer. "Howard was great," says Connick. "He had done a lot of stunt driving in some very big films and was a rally driver for years. He was very precise in his instructions as well."

"By lunchtime I was starting to enjoy it and looking forward to going out in the afternoon. I just wanted to get back in the car. I felt more in control. I'm a very bad passenger so the fact that I was driving the car and in control of my destiny relaxed me."

(from Seán's rally diary)

In the afternoon came the business end of the day: the time trial. A new course was mapped by the instructor: two or so miles of bone shuddering driving. Both drivers joked about needing a win, but it seems the politician's need was greater.

"I was very competitive this afternoon for the time trial. Everybody wants to be a winner. That competitive side was out in me again which I needed after the bloody election which was pretty soul destroying. For me, at the end, there was the sense that hey, I beat a world champion. It didn't matter that he was a world champion in snooker"

(from Seán's rally diary)

One second: that's the difference between triumph and failure. The difference between the politician and the snooker player. Neither driver knew who took the chequered flag until Howard broke the news. By then the engines had cooled and the champagne was ready to be uncorked.

Six months after his adventures in Saltburn and the general election, Seán Connick was still unemployed. Struggling to come to grips with his political defeat ("I spent months trying to adjust") he was confident that he would be back – after all it's not everyone who beats a world champion. "I don't effectively have a job because I moved away from business into politics," he says. "So I'll have to start all over again but I'm like most people at the moment. People are worried and facing huge challenges. Something will come up. I know it will."

Edel Reck's Guide to the Top Adaptive Sports Companies

*I*N THIS APPENDIX I want to share with you my tips and recommendations so that you, your family and your friends will have experiences to last a lifetime. I have personal experience of many of the listed activity providers while others have been recommended to me by colleagues.

Aviation

People with disabilities can now enjoy the freedom of being in the sky as many flying schools have sailplanes with hand controls. If a person is able to drive a car that has been adapted then they will also be able to fly a sailplane. This is absolute freedom because there are certainly no kerbs up there! I have not done sailplane gliding before but know of people who have and most of them began by contacting **Freedom's Wings International** whose HQ is in Coopersburg, Pennsylvania.

Website: www.freedomswings.org

Closer to home there is the **Ulster Gliding Club** which is located at Bellarena airfield, 366 Seacoast Rd., Co Londonderry.

Website: www.ulsterglidingclub.org
T: Jim Weston at +28-70358196
Email: jamesweston@btinternet.com

Canoeing, Kayaking, Rafting

Adaptive paddling simply means using the standard equipment which is adapted as needed to compensate for any function the paddler has lost due to disability. While an adaptation may be made to the paddle grip or the seating support within the craft, the sport of paddling is not changed or adapted. Canoes, kayaks and paddling gear are used in the same manner. Adaptive paddling programs are committed to providing full integration of paddlers who have a disability and to provide all with the equipment, teaching style and paddling locations that meets their needs. On the water everyone is equal. It's ability not disability that counts.

EB Adventures

EB Adventures pursue a policy of full inclusion for people with a disability to partake in their programs. They specialise in kayaking, whitewater rafting and trekking. If rugged outdoor experiences are your thing then this definitely is for you.

Website: www.ebadventures.com
T: Ed Bassett at +44 (7742) 826 977
Email: edbassettcanoe@aol.com

Savage Wilderness Safaris

Savage Wilderness Safaris work in conjunction with EB Adventures to provide some of the best whitewater rafting and trekking experiences in Kenya.
Website: whitewaterkenya.com

The Calvert Trust

The Calvert Trust has over thirty years experience in delivery exciting and challenging adventures to people of all abilities at three different centres in the UK – Exmoor, Kielder and the Lake District. The activities include water sports, horseback riding and ropes courses.

Website: www.calvert-trust.org.uk
T: +44 (1768) 772 255 (The Lake District)

Environmental Traveling Companions

ETC is based in San Francisco. It opens up the beauty and challenge of wilderness adventures to everyone, regardless of physical ability or financial limitations. Every year over 2000 people join ETC to raft whitewater rivers, sea kayak the waters of the Golden Gate and sleep beneath the open sky. A favourite of mine is a sea kayaking adventure in the azure waters of Baja California, Mexico

Website: www.etctrips.org
T: +1 (415) 474 7662
Email: info@etctrips.org

Common Ground Adventures

Based in Logan Utah, CGA's mission is to empower people to realise their full potential. You can choose to raft Grand Tetan National Park, camp in Glacier

National Park Montana or the Grand Canyon, Arizona (my favourite) or go classic camping in Canyonlands along Colorado's riverbanks. In the winter they head up to Jackson Hole, Wyoming for dogsledding adventures.

Website: www.cgadventures.org
T: +1 (435) 713 0288
Email: programs@cgadventures.org

Eco-Adventure International
Eco-Adventure International offer, among many other pursuits, canoeing. An unique trip is Tamshiyacu-Tahuayo Reserve which is situated along the upper tributaries of the Amazon River. There is no itinerary so you decide when and what you want to do. There are lots to choose from and I certainly recommend a jungle survival course. You can also swim with rare pink dolphins, go canoeing, bird watching, fishing and ziplining. You can even book your own personal guide if you want and the staff are really accommodating and helpful.

Website: www.eaiadventure.com
T: 1-800 –710 9453
Email: info@eaiadventure.com

Dogsledding

Dogsledding is an adventure activity where dogs are hitched to a sled for transportation across snow and ice. There are so many places in the world to have a really exciting experience, some more suitable to people with a disability than others.

The *Two for the Road* dog sledding episode with Sharon and Niall was shot in **Norway** at **Villmark Lodge**.

Website: www.nollert.no
T:+ 47 97178785
Email: booking@villmark.info

Or alternatively you can contact Villmark Lodge via the German office:
Andreas Uhrlandt
Heppenheimer Weg 50
D – 40227 Düsseldorf
T: +49 (211) 60 24 325
Email: andreas@villmark.info

Rocky Mountain Adaptive Sports Center
My favourite dogsledding program is run by the Rocky Mountain Adaptive Sports Center who are based in Calgary, Canada. Here you can choose to camp out in the snow or stay in a lodge. Lake Louise is spectacular in the Winter time.
Website: www.rmasc.ca

T: +1 (403) 675 9000
Email: info@rmasc.ca

Common Ground Adventures (*see previous page for contact details*) also run dogsledding trips in **Jackson Hole,** Wyoming.

The Adaptive Sports Center

The ASC in Crested Butte, Colorado is a non-profit organization that provides year round recreation activities, including adaptive skiing, snowboarding and ice climbing, mountain biking, abseiling, rock-climbing, horseback riding, dogsledding, ropes course (zipline) and sailing. It has a number of excellent programmes with highly qualified and motivated staff. Highly recommended.

Website: www.adaptivesports.org
T: +1 (970) 349 2296
Email: info@adaptivesports.org

Wintergreen Dogsled Lodge is based in Ely, Minnesota.
Website: www.dogsledding.com
T: +1 (218) 365-6022
Email: info@dogsledding.com

Hang Gliding and Paragliding

Hang gliding is flying prone with the wings above you. Being prone means that speed and performance is increased compared to being in a seated position. With the wings above you there is nothing to block your view below but because the view is obstructed above, many have semi transparent sails.

Paragliders are fully seated in their harness with feet first. A person's body obstructs the view below but the view above is much better than that of a hang glider.

The ASC, Telluride Adaptive Sports Program, Shaka Surf Retreat, Common Ground Adventures all have Hang Gliding and Paragliding included in their programs. Many people, including those who have disabilities, enjoy this activity. They start off paragliding in tandem with an instructor but some go on to fly solo.

Flyability

Flyability, which is based in Leicester, England, is the Disability Initiative of the British Hang Gliding & Paragliding Association.

Website: www.flyability.org.uk
T: +44 (1768) 773 040
Email: John-Crosbie@Flyability.org.uk

Horseriding

Stagecoach Trails Guest Ranch

Stagecoach Trails has the unique ability to offer a completely barrier-free horse riding holiday to all travellers and their families. They provide a program that is second to none. Each program is tailored to an individual's needs and abilities. For me this was a first and it was also a revelation. I was nervous at the start of the week but by the end I had really gained confidence. At STGR there's a real homely atmosphere with very helpful staff.
Website: www.stgr.com
T: +1 (928) 7278270
Email: vacation@stgr.com

Rancho Las Cascadas

Maeve and Sinéad went horseriding at Rancho las Cascadas in Mexico.
Website: www.ranchomex.com
T: Uschi at +52 (155) 30 360 390
Email: uschi@ranchomex.com
NB This property may not be suitable to some who have mobility issues.

Alpine Alternatives Alaska

Alpine Alternatives, Alaska, offers equestrian programs and week long summer camps with particular emphasis on serving school-going children and youth.
Website: alpinealternatives.org/programs.html
T: 1(907) 561 6655
Email: info@alpinealternatives.org

Motorbiking

Conquest International

Conquest International have invented a wheelchair-accessible motorbike whereby those who use chairs can sit in them, wheel up and take off to their hearts content. Check out their website for stockists in the UK. If you prefer to be a passenger there are opportunities to hire a bike with sidecars fitted.

Website: www.mobilityconquest.com

Wheel Adventures Sidecar Tours

Wheel Adventures Sidecar Tours are based in Queensland in Australia.
Website: www.wheeladventures.com.au
T: (431) 952516
Email: james@wheeladventures.com.au

Mountain Biking

Improvements in adaptive biking technology mean that it is now possible to offer riders with disabilities a genuine off-road experience. Like mountain biking on traditional bikes, gradients and trail features mean that a degree of nerve, skill and fitness may be required to successfully negotiate the various routes. It may be not everyone's cup of tea, but for some, myself included, it provides the means to get away from the paved environment, challenge ourselves physically and feel the adrenaline buzz of speed.

The Adaptive Sports Center (ASC), Colorado, where I went biking with Kamal, has a number of biking programmes. (*See contact details under dog sledding*)

Telluride Adaptive Sports

Telluride Adaptive Sports Program is dedicated to providing individuals with programs that include adaptive skiing, snowboarding and mountain biking. In recent years they have expanded their program to include ice climbing adventures in Alaska.

Website: www.tellurideadaptivesports.org
T: +1 (970) 728 5010
Email: tasp@tellurideadaptivesports.org

No Barriers USA

No Barriers USA organise a summit each year for activity providers and extreme sports enthusiasts alike. Here you can try almost every activity possible.

Here they provide hands-on clinics and product demonstrations for all to have a go. For the time of your life this is well worth checking out.

Website: www.nobarriersusa.org
T: +1 (952) 472 2400
Email: info@nobarriersusa.org

Roughriderz Downhill Mountain Bike Club

Roughriderz Downhill Mountain Bike Club, which is based in the UK, is the place for you if you are a thrill seeker. Roughriderz have 'Taster Days' for anybody willing to give it a go. It's an integrated club for people with and without a physical disability.

Website: www.roughriderz.co.uk
T:+ 44 (1772) 562883
Email: phil@roughriderz.co.uk

Rally driving

Cyclone Mobility is an organisation in East Yorkshire providing motoring enthusiasts the experience of driving a rally car. Anyone who can drive a car with hand controls will be able to drive a rally car because the controls are just the same. Just ask Seán and Ken after their TFTR adventure!

Website: cyclonemobility.com
T: Dave Hawkins at +44 (1964) 623 881
Email: info@cyclonemobility.com

Rockclimbing

Adaptive Rock Climbing is climbing using adaptive methods. Paraplegic rock climbers use chest harness for climbing and safety. Knee pads prevent climbers from scratching and injuring their knees while climbing. Everyone has to learn how their bodies work on the rock so it doesn't matter if someone has paraplegia, visual impairment or are minus a limb. It is very social and it can offer participants a great sense of achievement. It's also a great way to stay in shape.

There are many activity providers offering this extreme sport including the **Adaptive Sports Centre** and **Telluride Adaptive Sport** but my favourite in Europe is **Handixtreme** in Spain who offer this activity in the Pyrenees Mountains.

Website. www.handixtreme.com
T: +34 (607) 426 385
Email: info@handixtremecom

Other providers include:
Adaptive Sports Centre Colorado (*see under dog sledding for contact details*)
Telluride Adaptive Sports Program (*see under Mountain Biking for contact details*).

Sailing

Adaptive Sailing is an enhanced version of regular sailing that uses adaptive equipment to support various physical conditions to enable everyone to engage in another exhilarating sport. **Sailforce.ie, The Irish Disabled Sailing Association** (www.sailforce.ie) was founded in 1982. Its affiliation to the Irish Sailing Association gives it responsibility for the promotion and development of sailing in Ireland. Sailing can be an activity primarily for pleasure but some may have a desire to develop their competitive potential. The IDSA can facilitate these needs. Sailing can foster team spirit between able-bodied and disabled people. Both **Kinsale Yacht Club** and **Lough Derg Yacht Club** have good wheelchair access.

The Jubilee Sailing Trust
The Jubilee Sailing Trust (www.jst.org.uk) promotes diversity awareness and provides life changes for all including people with physical and sensory disabilities. Tallship sailing can give you a thrill and adventure of life at sea as Trevor and Eamonn discovered! *The Tenacious* and *Lord Nelson* (which played a big part in *Two For The Road*) are the only two tallships in the world which enables everyone to sail side-by-side as equals by taking the helm, setting sails, keeping watch etc.

Website: www.jst.org.uk
T: +44 (23) 8044 9108
Email: info@jst.org.uk

Scuba Diving

Adaptive scuba diving is a training philosophy that addresses the specific needs of a disabled individual, trains to their specific disability and prepares them to dive with mainstream divers in open waters. Adaptations are made so that everyone, regardless of circumstances, can safely learn to participate in scuba diving.

New Mexico Scuba Center
New Mexico Scuba Center is located in Albuquerque, NM. Its mission is to provide top quality scuba diving experiences to all disabled and able-bodied alike. Their goal is to produce competent and well trained divers. Divers with quadriplegia or visual impairment are trained as escorted divers.

Website: www.nmscuba.com
T: +1 (505) 271 0633
Email: nmscuba@qwestoffice.net

Dive Pirates Foundation
The Dive Pirates Foundation, which is based in Texas, was set up to train those with a disability to dive in open waters like their able-bodied counterparts. They have in the past run trips in the Bahamas and Cayman Islands.
Website: www.divepirates.org
T:+ 1 (877) 3933483
Email: divepirates@divepirates.org

Life Rolls On
Life Rolls On provides opportunities to people with a disability to dive at their own ability level. As a group they organise diving trips to exotic locations worldwide.

Website: liferollson.org
T: Kris S Nakamura – Executive Director is at +1 (310) 807 5488 – Ext 802
Email: Kris@LifeRollsOn.org

Norway Handicapped Scuba Association

The Norway Handicapped Scuba Association also facilitates diving for people with a physical disability.

Website: www.handikap.no
T: +47 (90) 222130
Email: kontakt@handikap.no

Skiing

Skiing for people with disabilities became popular after World War II with the return of injured veterans. It is both a recreational pastime and a competitive sport open to those with any manner of competitive or physical disability. Adaptations include the use of outriggers, skiing retention devices, sit skis like monoskis or biskis, high visibility instructor/guide bibs and inter skier communication systems or audible clues for blind skiers. A guide skier can assist the sit skier and this is known as bucketing. Recreational skiing programs for people with a disability exist at resorts across the globe.

Disability Snowsport UK

If you enjoy experiencing new things, love adventure and want to learn how to ski with like-minded people then DSUK might just be right for you. Each year they run a series of skiing and snowboarding weeks to some of Europe's and North America's resorts for individuals as well as tailor-made adventures for groups. If you are travelling by yourself that's no problem because many do. A favourite of mine is **La Plagne**. Give them a try and you'll never look back.

Website: www.disabilitysnowsport.org.uk
T: +44 (1479) 861272
Email: admin@disabilitysnowsport.org.uk

Breckenridge Outdoor Education Center (BOEC)

Deep in the heart of the Rocky Mountains is a unique place where their wilderness programs include whitewater rafting on the Colorado River, canoeing on the Labyrinth Canyon in Utah, sea kayaking on Lake Powell (my favourite) and lots more throughout the Rocky Mountains including handcycling, rock-climbing, wilderness camping, skiing and snowboarding. One great addition to BOEC is their very own onsite accessible, self catering lodge. Here you can meet fellow travellers and chill out.

Website: www.boec.org
T: + 1 (970) 4536422
Email: boec@boec.org

Adaptive Adventures

Adaptive Adventures run programs for all seasons from skiing and snowboarding in winter to waterskiing and wakeboarding in the summer. Their Center has offices in Chicago and Colorado.

Website: www.adaptiveadventures.org
T: +1 (303) 679 2770 (Colorado) or +1 (847) 251 8445 Chicago)
Email: colorado info@adaptiveadventures.org
or joel@adaptiveadventures.org

The United States Adaptive Recreation Center.

This organisation takes to the waters of nearby Big Bear Lake, California, and to the mountains in summer and winter for lots of thrills and spills. Their mission is to ensure that the outdoors is available to all. Their programs include waterskiing, jet skiing, kayaking, sailing, mountain biking, skiing.

Website: www.usarc.org
T: +1 (909) 584 0269
Email: mail@usarc.org

Totalskidskolan is a very good adaptive ski program in Sweden.
Website: www.totalskidskolan.z.se
T: 46 647 53777
Email: bokningen.@total.skidskolan.se

Snorkelling

Snorkelling allows a swimmer to see sea life underwater. Minimum equipment and training is required.

Roll Over Bali

Roll Over Bali is run by Claudia Kurz and provides individually tailored wheelchair suitable tours and holidays in Bali. It does not cater for groups.

Website: www.rolloverbali.tripod.com
T:+ 62 (361) 733805
Email: inquires@rolloverbail.com

Surfing

Shaka Surf Retreat

Frank Bauer, co-founder of Shaka Surf Retreat in Costa Rica, runs adaptive surf camps throughout the year for people of all abilities. Here you are spoilt for choice when it comes to adrenaline pumped activities. Besides surfing you can choose to go ziplining, waterfall rappelling, horseriding through rivers, jungles and lots more. This resort with infinite possibilities is top class.

Website: www.shakacostarica.com
T: 1 (506) 240 1118
Email: shakacr@gmail.com

Ocean Healing Group

OHG's motto is 'carving the 'dis' out of disability' and this non-profit organisation, based at Aspen, Colorado, is dedicated to providing adaptive sport adventure (surfing, ziplining, diving, etc) to mobility impaired young people and their parents.

Website: www.oceanhealinggroup.org
T: 1 (970) 3799811
Email: guest@oceanhealinggroup.org

Trekking

Trekking is the practice of taking multi day hikes through rugged terrain where common means of transport is not available. The Himalayan routes are famous for attracting large numbers. Many activity providers now offer this activity to people with a disability in places like Peru, Patagonia and the Himalayas.

Apumayo Expeditions

Apumayo Expeditions is based in Lima, Peru and specialises in trekking adventures along the ancient ruins of Machu Picchu. You can also experience the vast Andean landscapes, go horseback riding, hot-air ballooning, kayaking on Lake Titicaca (highest lake in the World) with guides who are highly trained in safety, rescue and first aid. This is a trip of a lifetime but be prepared for some and perhaps lots of manhandling. Improvisation may also be required. Bearing these in mind I still highly recommend this trip.

Website: www.apumayo.com
T: +51 84246018
Email: contact@apumayo.com

Able To Travel

Able to Travel makes ground arrangements for travellers with a disability from trekking in the Galapagos Island to the jungles of the Amazon.

Website: www.abletotravel.org
T: 1 (888) 211 3635
Email: info@abletotravel.org

Ability Adventures

This New Zealand-based company (HQ at Dunedin) customises itineraries to clients interests, needs and budgets. Whether your preference is to experience adrenaline-pumping activities, rainforests or different cultures, Ability Adventures can arrange it all from trekking to river rafting, sky diving to bungee jumping.

Website: www.abilityadventures.co.nz
T: +64 (3) 476 2013
Email: info@abilityadventures.co.nz

Sam McConnell Desert Expeditions

Sam Mc Connell Desert Expeditions work closely with EB Adventures to run trips for people with mixed abilities and backgrounds. These include the Namib Desert, Sinai Desert, Jordan etc.

Website: www.sam-mcconnell-expeditions.com
T: + 44 (7826) 292632
Email: info@sam-mcconnell-expeditions.com

Ziplining

A Zipline consist of a pulley suspended on a cable mounted to an incline. In order to be propelled by gravity, the incline has to be fairly steep. They come in many forms most often used as a means to entertainment. They enable the user to be propelled by gravity to travel from top to bottom of the inclined cable by using or attaching to the moving pulley. **The Adaptive Sports Centre in Crested Butte, Colorado** lists this as an activity in their summer programme and **Shaka Surf Retreat** also can organise tours through the rainforests of Costa Rica.

General travel websites

There are a number of other general travel websites that I would highly recommend. These include **www.able-travel.com**, **www.access-able.com** and **www.rollingrains.com**. You also check out the blog **Rolling Rains Report.** **Nellida Barbeito** is an advocate for inclusive tourism in South America. The website listed below is in Spanish but Nellida speaks fluent English and will get back to anyone within 24 hours.

mail: nelbarbi@hotmail.com and nbarbeito@ttsviajes.com

http://nelidabarbeito.blogspot.com/2009/01/accessible-traveling-services-in.html

http://www.ttsviajes.com/viajes-turismo-con-discapacidad.php

Thorn Tree Forum has a thread for disabled travellers on **www.lonely-planet.com**